". . . FOR
THE LEAST OF MY
BROTHERS"

"... FOR THE LEAST OF MY BROTHERS"

The Spirituality of Mother Teresa and Catherine Doherty

*

OMER TANGHE

Translated from the Flemish
by Jean Mac Donald

ALBA · HOUSE   NEW · YORK

SOCIETY OF ST. PAUL, 2187 VICTORY BLVD., STATEN ISLAND, NEW YORK 10314

Original Title: *Calcutta Brieven*
Published by: Publications Lanoo, Tielt, Belgium

Library of Congress Cataloging-in-Publication Data

Tanghe, Omer, 1928-
    [Calcutta brieven. English]
    For the least of my brothers : the spirituality of Mother Teresa
  and Catherine Doherty / Omer Tanghe.
       p.   cm.
    Translation of: Calcutta brieven.
    ISBN 0-8189-0565-4
    1. Spirituality — Catholic Church — History — 20th century.
  2. Teresa, Mother, 1910- 3. Doherty, Catherine de Hueck, 1900- .
  4. Catholic Church — Doctrines — History — 20th century. I. Title.
BX2350.65.T36   1989   89-38220
248'.092'2 — dc20   CIP

Designed, printed and bound in the United States of
America by the Fathers and Brothers of the
Society of St. Paul, 2187 Victory Boulevard,
Staten Island, New York 10314, as part of their
communications apostolate.

Printing Information:

Current Printing - first digit 1 2 3 4 5 6 7 8 9 10 11 12

Year of Current Printing - first year shown
1989   1990   1991   1992   1993   1994   1995   1996

PREFACE

This collection of letters from Calcutta is the culmination of a year's contact with Mother Teresa and her Missionaries of Charity. When I became Director of the Mission Aid Societies in my Diocese of Bruges, my predecessor, Canon Jose Lowie (1898-1979) asked me to devote special attention to both the Lievans Mission in India and the Archdiocese of Galilee in Israel.

The Lievans Mission, in what is now the Archdiocese of Ranchi, has blossomed into one of the most promising churches of the world. Its seeds were sown by the Flemish Jesuit, Constant Lievans, in 1885. It was lovingly cultivated during the ensuing hundred years by a long line of Flemish and Dutch Missionaries. The Ranchi Mission in Chotanagpur was originally a part of the Calcutta Mission in West Bengal.

"In Ranchi, as in Calcutta, lie the roots of our missionary efforts; I beg you do not neglect this mission," was Jose's plea. How could I turn a deaf ear to it? So, since 1968, I have made regular trips to Calcutta and Ranchi endeavoring to strengthen the bonds already existing between our church communities.

It was inevitable that sooner or later I would cross paths with Mother Teresa. She begged me repeatedly to help with the spiritual direction of her Sisters, as well as the spiritual growth of our own priests. During these twenty years, Mother Teresa's spirituality has become a source of inspiration and strength for my own priestly life.

Canon Lowie also cherished, in a very special way, what he called "Jesus' Church" in the Holy Land. Before he resigned, he introduced me to the Greek-Melkite Catholic Archbishop of Galilee, Bishop Joseph Raya. The latter invited me to help bring about a collaboration between him and our local Flemish Church. "To manifest the face of God to those entrusted to our care," he said. Archbishop Raya was a member of Madonna House in Combermere, Ontario in Canada. He taught me to know Catherine Doherty, the foundress of a training center for the lay apostolate. "It is called Madonna House," he said, and he told me that there priests and laity live and work together.

Catherine Doherty died in 1985, leaving behind an important heritage of books and writings about her spirituality. She is considered one of the most promising spiritual writers of this century. With Mother Teresa she can also be considered one of the greatest and saintliest women of our 20th century. One of the best known of her books is entitled *Poustinia* (Ave Maria Press, 1975). In this book she really challenges modern man to become a contemplative in the *poustinia* of his own heart. *Poustinia* is the Russian word for *desert*.

Thanks to Archbishop Raya, I have been privileged to visit Catherine regularly since the early '70s. In 1976, I was honored to become a member of her spiritual family as an associate priest. She also helped and inspired me as a priest to have a great love for Jesus and Mary and to serve them more perfectly in the Church.

Not long ago, during some days of recollection in Mother Teresa's house in Calcutta, I was able to explain the Little Mandate of Madonna House to more than 400

Missionaries of Charity, and we meditated upon it together. There is a remarkable similarity in the teachings and spirituality of Catherine Doherty and Mother Teresa.

From a direct contact with Mother Teresa and the outstanding reality of Calcutta, I was able to compare the Little Mandate of Catherine Doherty and the "I Thirst" spirituality of Mother Teresa in these letters. They were not written for fictitious persons, but to real friends at home and abroad. These include: a journalist, a parish priest, a doctor, foster parents, a missionary, an archbishop, a Carmelite nun, a young nurse, the Missionary Sisters of Charity in Ghent, and a staff member of Madonna House in Paris. Every letter treats of one of Mother Teresa's sayings and compares it to a similar message found in Catherine Doherty's Little Mandate.

Since I will be quoting this Little Mandate, it might be well to pause for a moment and explain why it is so important in speaking of the spirituality of Catherine Doherty and why it means so much to the Apostolate which she has founded. I can best do this by quoting what Father Robert Wild of Madonna House says in his book, *Journey to the Lonely Christ* (Alba House, New York, 1987):

> The words of the Mandate did not drop ready-made from Heaven, but grew in her mind and heart over the years. . . .
> In one sense Catherine's spiritual life can be seen as the deeper and deeper understanding and living out of the meaning of these words of the Mandate, spoken by the Lord to her in the depths of her being. My own study of the Mandate has convinced me that these are not rationally thought out words, but real intuitions of the Spirit. These words are simply in her, and she does not need to think them up each time she wishes to speak. They are in

her like the very air she breathes. When she breathes breath comes out of her mouth. So when she speaks about her spirituality, the words of the Mandate come out of her heart. They are her very life. I quote them here in full:

Arise — go! Sell all you possess. Give it directly, personally to the poor. Take up My cross (their cross) and follow Me — going to the poor — being poor — being one with them — one with Me.

Little — be always little. . . simple — poor — child-like.

Preach the Gospel WITH YOUR LIFE — WITHOUT COMPROMISE — listen to the Spirit — he will lead you.

Do little things exceedingly well for love of Me.

Love — love — love, never counting the cost.

Go into the marketplace and stay with Me . . . pray . . . fast . . . pray always . . . fast.

Be hidden — be a light to your neighbor's feet. Go without fear into the depths of men's hearts . . . I shall be with you.

Pray always. I WILL BE YOUR REST.

In Calcutta, I could spend long hours in discussion with Mother Teresa about the "marketplace of the heart" that must be emptied in order to be filled with God; about Jesus who wants to be our whole life; about this suffering Jesus in the sick and the poor; about the necessity for childlikeness and simplicity, if one is to accomplish something beautiful for God; about the heart of evangelization, which is to proclaim and praise God's thirst for mankind and mankind's for God; about love for the Eucharist; about love, faith and contemplation as characteristics of a God-centered life; about life commitment and vocation; about the irreplaceable role of Mary, who helps us purify our hearts and lives for Jesus.

I wanted to write about these essentials, as Catherine Doherty always called them, in my letters from Calcutta. They are separate reflections that one can read at random. They are an expression of my gratitude to both Mother Teresa and Catherine Doherty, who have helped me in my priestly life during the course of twenty years. They have helped me grow ever more and more in love with God and to live through Mary for Jesus alone.

They contain, at the same time, a sincere and personal witness for the many friends to whom I dedicate this book.

Omer Tanghe

CONTENTS

INTRODUCTION

Dear Omer,

It is with more than the usual interest that I read your letters. I am convinced that this book will find a broad public, and I hope sincerely that many young people will discover it. One can't ignore the fact that so many of them, for whom the Church has so little to offer these days, are full of admiration for people such as Mother Teresa and Catherine Doherty, whose spirituality you have so beautifully described here and in your book, *As I Have Loved You* (Veritas Publications, Dublin, 1988).

These radically evangelical ideals still exert a powerful attraction. It would be wrong to limit them to a one-sided interest in the social or horizontal dimension of Christianity. Young people realize all too well that there are people "for whom" one can live, but that — to give a lasting meaning — there must be a something (Someone) *from whom* one can live. And that is why that same group shows such an interest in the purely contemplative life. Perhaps it would be good if the pilgrimage to Katmandu, so popular in the '60s, would be interrupted by a sojourn in Calcutta, where one could experience a true broadening of one's awareness. This would be done by plunging oneself, with eyes wide open, into a radical self-commitment to the poor.

These last years I have repeatedly discerned that a Christian can only stand out among others in this world by a radical living out of the evangelical values. This differentiates, in practice, the Christian from people who practice any of the world's other great religions. You know that I have always had the greatest respect, even admiration, for these religions and for the cultures and civilizations that give rise to them. But a deeper knowledge of them also teaches one their limitations. In the refugee camps of Asia, for example, I have often seen that those who try to alleviate, in a concrete way, the needs of these rudderless, displaced people are persons who are animated by an evangelical inspiration.

I remember the story of several boat people on the Malayan seal island, Pulau Bidong. After their boat was boarded by Thai pirates and they were robbed of their last possessions (literally frisked for anything that might be taken), and severely manhandled, some of them were thrown into the sea. The survivors bobbed around on the South China Sea without any direction, in a state of absolute stupor.

Suddenly a fishing boat pulled alongside. The refugees thought that they were to be the prey of yet another harassment (it happens often enough), but no, they proved to be Thai fishermen who, in Buddha's name, offered the starving people fish from their own catch. There was undoubtedly much courage needed for the Thai fishermen to extend this humanitarian gesture in view of the hostile attitude prevailing in their region towards these Vietnamese boat people.

When I heard this account in Malaya, I thought of the Gospel story in which the Lord fed a huge crowd on a handful of fish and bread which He multiplied. Perhaps the meaning of this miraculous multiplication is this: that the

Christian does not settle for a sensational, onetime only act of philanthropy, but is creative enough to continue carrying out that "wonder." In other words, that he, more than any other in our society, irrespective of social position, feels himself responsible for the poor, the displaced, those without direction — the marginals. This, in my opinion, is the heart of Christianity. I have slowly, but ever so surely, arrived at this conclusion.

A sustained altruism should always be characteristic of Christians. In my life and during the course of my career, I have met a few people who managed to succeed in forgetting themselves completely in their commitment to the poor. This is the turning point, the metanoia. It had totally transformed these people. I recall that, during King Baudouin's visit to Bangladesh, he met a nun who worked among the lepers — people who literally have nothing — no material possessions whatever. Some scarcely had even a body. The nun, who shared their lives twenty-four hours out of twenty-four uninterruptedly during so many years, had reached such a degree of detachment that it certainly signified the total conversion of her life. In a talk she let it slip that her only concern was that at her death she be buried under an old oak tree that she had already chosen. She said, "And preferably deep enough because I still find it ghastly — even after all these years — to see so many bodies washed up with the yearly floods because the people continue to dig such shallow graves."

Dear Omer, not long ago, a sort of epigram from the Roman poet Catullus caught my attention: *Odi et amo. Quare id faciam, fortasse requiris? Nescio, sed fieri sentio et excrucior.* "I hate and I love. Why is that so, I ask you? I do not know. I feel it, it is so, I bear it. I feel myself crucified." The poet lived about fifty years before Christ. They both died at about the same age. But this Jesus of Nazareth, who lived a half century later, was in reality crucified because He alone had loved to the bitter end.

I am convinced that your letters from Calcutta will not only speak to many people, but will also show the reader the way to Him who inspired Mother Teresa and Catherine Doherty to follow such unusual calls. Only you who knows the minds of these two exceptional women so well could write this. That's why I would like to say to everyone, "Take and read!"

With warm affection,

Marcel Van Nieuwenborgh, Chairman,
Scriptores Christiani

LETTER I:
CALCUTTA IS EVERYWHERE

To Mark, Journalist

Calcutta, December 2, 1987

Dear Mark,

As I write this letter I am sitting in the comfortable guest room of the residence of Archbishop Henry D'Souza. It is built in the high, colonial style so popular in former years. Evening has already settled in.

This afternoon Father Laborde compared India to a banyan tree. From his parish, skirting the Pilkana slums in Howrah, we went to see the famous botanical gardens of Calcutta situated on the western banks of the Hooghly River. The park, which extends some 20 kilometers (12.5 miles) inland, was laid out by the East India Company in 1787 and has, as its most spectacular attraction, a banyan tree which is two centuries old. It is said to be the broadest and rarest tree in the world. You aren't sure whether it is a tree or a cluster as it is impossible to differentiate the trunk from the long, broad branches.

"This is Calcutta! Such is India!" Laborde exclaimed. This priest is one of the main characters in the well-known book, *City of Joy*, written by the French journalist and novelist, Dominique Lapierre. It depicts the life of the slums. Calcutta has 3,000 such areas. Lapierre wrote about the Pilkana slums in particular.

In order to preserve a measure of anonymity Father Laborde was called Father Lambert in the book. Under the influence of what he saw, Lapierre wrote:

> Here, in the heart of this underworld, I encounter more heroism, more love, more desire to share, more joy, and ultimately more happiness than in most cities of our rich western world. I meet people who have literally nothing and yet possess everything. Amidst the shadows, the mire and the excretion, I discover more beauty and expectation than I do in our so-called paradises. Above all, I discover that this inhuman city brings forth, magically as it were, saints — Mother Teresa, of course, but also next-to-unknown saints such as Father Lambert, the Frenchman who came to help, and to stand side by side with the destitute.

> I have slept in Lambert's hovel, a one by two meter space, without either ventilation or lighting, overrun by rats and cockroaches and where, after every rainfall, you almost expire from the overwhelming stench of urine. . . .

Francis Laborde is now 61 years old. He is a member of the Prado in Paris. The Prado is a community of priests and religious founded to help the poor. He lives in a small, dark house built next to the Church of Nirmala Mata Maria Girja Parish on Andul Road, in the heavily populated area of the Howrah district. I went to see him at the request of Father

Celest Van Exem, the 78-year-old Flemish Jesuit who was a pastor for many years in one of the parishes of Howrah and who directed Mother Teresa from the very beginning of the foundation of the Missionaries of Charity. Francis Laborde is a thin, slightly-built man with an ascetic face. His shaky English betrays his French origins. I was thoughtless enough to mention that I had read Lapierre's book, but I was quickly silenced by his retort that he found all the publicity that was given him in it pure rubbish.

The book had become a best-seller, and it made Lapierre famous. The royalties from his author's rights and the other funds raised from the Pilkana projects have proved to be quite substantial and extremely helpful. However, Laborde is clearly annoyed with the publicity and would have preferred to remain anonymous as a simple priest present among the poorest of the poor — these poor refugees who huddle together in Howrah. They are Adibasis from Chotanagpur who came to seek their fortune in the big city and became stranded there. They are children of misery. Many of them are handicapped. These are his parishioners.

Laborde spoke forcefully: "It is from their reality that we must truly experience our priesthood. One mustn't theorize too much about their situation or write exciting stories. One must simply stand in their midst with the Heart of Jesus. One must share their life, be concerned with their lot and listen to the crying needs of their poverty."

He showed me his church. It is rather cozy and accommodates 300 persons. There are no chairs or benches and the Blessed Sacrament is reserved in a side chapel. Before the tabernacle I saw Andre Roublev's icon of the Trinity. Laborde knelt on both knees before the icon and remained so for quite a while. Spontaneously my thoughts turned to Mother Teresa whom I had so often seen praying in this same position. Francois Laborde is assisted in his pastoral work by a few Indian Sisters of Prado and by Missionary Brothers of Charity who live in the sprawling and ugly adjacent premises among the mentally and physically handicapped. Further on, in a side street, Father Laborde runs another house where still more handicapped are cared for by a handful of generous women. "Among these lay helpers are Muslims, Christians and Hindus," he told me. "All are witnesses of God's Love."

In a remote corner of his parish, he has arranged quarters for countless Adibasi families from the area of Ranchi. Originally they were settled in the slums. Laborde collected as much money as he could from friends and well-wishers and built stone houses for them. Most of them are Catholic. He goes there regularly to celebrate Mass for them and to chat with them. The people welcomed us with genuine and simple warmth. Their catechist showed us around. The loving courtesy these poor people show their visitors left a deep and indelible impression on me.

At the end of our visit, we made our way to the botanical gardens. Laborde confided to me that he had actually come to Calcutta twenty years earlier with the intention of gathering material for his doctorate in social anthropology, focusing on the mentality and lifestyle of the slum residents. "I quickly forgot my academic ambitions and decided to remain with them, living and working as a priest," he said. He went on: "I know that many say that Calcutta is more than the poor, the slums, and the charitable work of Mother Teresa. This is quite possible, but it is no excuse to evade the reality as if one were blind. The poor do exist; you just cannot ignore them."

As do many others in this huge city, Laborde belongs to the group of saints that Lapierre wrote about. There are parish priests, Brothers and Sisters of Mother Teresa, missionaries of various congregations and orders, countless women religious and lay helpers who amaze you and move you. Lapierre wrote about them. These people immediately teach you to discover the beating heart of this city and the millions who live and die here.

Monsignor Leander Da Costa, who was my chauffeur, drove me back to the archbishop's residence on Park Street. It is just next to St. Xavier's University College, which is under the direction of Belgian Jesuits. You know that I have often come to Calcutta during the course of the last twenty years to meet with groups of missionary friends on their way to the Lievens Mission in Ranchi where about 60 Flemish Jesuits work as missionaries. In this way I have grown quite familiar with the profile of Calcutta. And yet, even today, as I look out over this sprawling city, I am continually amazed at the sea of people who overflow the alleys, the back streets, the various quarters, the avenues, the roads and the paths like a swelling flood of humanity.

It has rained and the wintry weather of these early December days is chilly. The slums and hovels look even more miserable and dingy than usual. The better homes in the residential areas (especially those from colonial days) have lost their glamor forever. I saw wash hanging outside myriads of crammed flats in buildings ten to twenty stories high. The facades, discolored by the humid, tropical weather, look leprous. A thousand blaring cars fight their way through the throngs of people. It all makes you dizzy, and your thoughts turn spontaneously to your customary western comforts and the luxurious hotels of Calcutta — to the "Grand," as the 5-star hotel, the "Oberoi Grand" on Jawaharal Nehru Street, is commonly called. There the rich, foreign tourists lodge. They sip cool drinks and try to forget the trauma of Calcutta, try to recover from the oppressing culture shock. In the "Grand's" publicity pamphlet I read:

Calcutta — India's largest city, former capital of the British Raj, and the intellectual nerve center of the subcontinent.

A great, sprawling megalopolis of 8 million people that would be impossible were it not real. A city beyond description; certainly beyond censure or praise. It is simply Calcutta.

Frustrating and demanding, yet still vigorous, Calcutta is a centre for contemporary theatre and cinema, for passionate art, articulate literature and extraordinary music.

Calcutta is a city with a soul; a city which will demand your attention in a way no other city can match.

Calcutta is the very essence of India!

Leander had been scrutinizing my face during the course of our rodeo-like ride through the city center and over the steel bridge which spanned the Hooghly River. He must have noticed my confusion for he said, "You get used to it, you know. It won't be long before you, too, will love this city."

Da Costa took care that I also saw the "other side" of Calcutta. In the late afternoon we went to St. Paul's Cathedral, one of the most beautiful churches in all of India. It is next to the Victoria Memorial and the botanical gardens, and is one of the main tourist attractions. There we enjoyed what proved to be a most unique concert.

Imagine for a moment that the British had transported their most imposing buildings and monuments, in the typical style of the Empire, from the center of London to Calcutta. This Anglican church is an impressive and charming building, and the Indians are very proud of it.

Johann Sebastian Bach's *Magnificat in D* and Wolfgang Amadeus Mozart's *Coronation Mass* were on the program, which was executed by the Calcutta Chamber Orchestra and the Calcutta Choir — thirty-five musicians and forty-five vocalists. The church was packed with members of the diplomatic corps and Calcutta's upper class.

"Bach and Mozart in Calcutta!" Leander whispered to me ecstatically. "All of the musicians are amateurs who have reached a high degree of professional competence. Listen to how well they handle the Latin even though most of them are Hindus." He pointed to the text in the program:

> It is at once clear that the *Magnificat* is a cry of triumph — God's triumph! Mary knows that God is using her, and Bach's aim is to bring home to us that God wants each of us to turn the world upside down — by removing the scandal of the poverty which afflicts at least 80% of the world's population. . . .

That gripped me forcibly! So did the songs, the music, and the audience of music lovers who were obviously deeply religious people. It had the same effect on my confrere, Leander, who, during the singing of the *Credo*, could not restrain his tears at the words: "et crucifixus est sub Pontio Pilato, passus et sepultus est." This is Calcutta! I thought again of Francois Laborde and of the saintly people, each in his or her own way, who *live* the *Magnificat* and the *Credo* in Pilkana and in the other slums of this vast city. My first visit to Calcutta and my first meeting with Mother Teresa wedged its way into my mind.

Because of the heavy monsoon rains and thunder storms, the Lufthansa direct flight that had brought us from Frankfort to Calcutta suffered delays and we missed our connecting flight. Consequently we were put up in the "Grand."

The following morning I looked out from the hotel lobby at all that was transpiring before my eyes. Right in front of the entrance, I saw a young woman shabbily dressed — an outcast, an untouchable. She was sitting on the sidewalk with the body of a child in her lap. A few moments later, some Sisters of Mother Teresa came by and, ever so gently, helped the woman to her feet and took the little corpse with them. This was my first contact with the Missionaries of Charity. The doorman, a robust Sikh with beard, turban and a white waistcoat with red shoulder pieces, had stood calmly watching my reaction to what was going on. He then asked if I knew those Sisters. When I shook my head, he said, "You should if you're a Catholic. They are the Sisters of Mother Teresa."

"Who is this Mother Teresa?" I inquired.

"She is the angel of Calcutta, sir," he replied with utter conviction. "You definitely must meet her."

And so I determined to do just that. I went to their motherhouse located in the Lower Circular Road to see her and to speak with her. Since then I have met her on various occasions both in Calcutta and in Europe. She asked me to work with her in imparting a greater awareness of what it means to live one's vocation as a priest or religious today — to live wholly and totally for Jesus through Mary, and thereby to help alleviate Jesus' thirst for the poor and their own crying need for God. I spoke with her again in Rome and spent many hours with her during the retreat I preached in July of 1985 in the little house of her Sisters working in Northern Europe.

In the beginning of October of the following year, she came to Flanders for a few days to visit with Father Celest Van Exem, S.J. He was back in his hometown of Elveridge for a vacation after an absence of eighteen years. He had come home to recuperate from an operation. She was also the guest of the Diocese of Hasselt and of Dr. Jan Gysen of Genk. Needless to say, she left a strong and deep impression on everyone by her mere presence and simple words.

During our meetings, she had repeatedly urged me to come to Calcutta to preach days of recollection to her Missionaries of Charity about what it means to live a God-centered life. Very early this morning in her house on Lower Circular Road, we were actually discussing the program for these long-anticipated days of recollection. We spoke about Calcutta.

"Calcutta is everywhere," she said. "We can discover Calcutta with its misery and sin everywhere, Father. Only then will we realize that we are all destined for higher, nobler things. The things that we often allow to clutter our hearts can only serve to intensify our thirst for Jesus. This thirst is the poverty in which we all must live."

I saw how her eyes were fixed on the cross that I wore around my neck — a simple, metal cross with the words "Pax-Caritas" (Peace-Love). This cross is worn by the members of Madonna House and identifies us as belonging to the spiritual movement, the Lay Apostolate founded by Catherine Doherty. It is called the Madonna House Apostolate.

"Catherine Doherty and her spirituality are not unknown to me," Mother Teresa said. "Speak to my Sisters about them."

That, my dear Mark, is the reason for my being in Calcutta now. I am here to speak about and give witness to the *poustinia* of the heart in which you also have to interpret Calcutta. In letters to friends in Flanders and around the world I want to tell how I was able to experience this with Mother Teresa and her Sisters, with Leander, Francois

Laborde and the many saintly people whom I found in this "City of Joy."

It will be a while yet before I will be able to fall asleep. My mind keeps going over the past day spent in the slums of Howrah, in the house of Mother Teresa and in St. Paul's Cathedral. "This is Calcutta! Such is India!" Laborde had said these things to me when he showed me the banyan tree, the gigantic tree without a trunk. "You don't know where it begins or where it ends."

I can still hear Mother Teresa saying to me, "Calcutta is everywhere, present in the heart of the people. . . ." And the words of the Little Mandate of Catherine Doherty — words that her spiritual family try to live by, words that she considered to be those of Jesus himself to her, came to mind:

> Go into the marketplace and stay with Me. . . .
> Go without fear into the depths of men's hearts. . . .
> I shall be with you. . . .

I have just closed the shutters before the door and windows of my guest room to keep out the chill evening wind from the Gulf of Bengal. It blows over this hot, tropical land and numbs the people who live on the sidewalks under the open skies or under a tarpaulin and muffles the noise of the ever-honking cars.

This is Calcutta, dear Mark. I wish you a peaceful night.

Omer

LETTER II:

LET JESUS BE YOUR WHOLE LIFE

To Jos, Parish Priest

Calcutta, December 4, 1987

Dear Jos,

A few weeks ago on World Mission Sunday, you invited me to preach in your church about our responsibility to evangelize the world. Between the various Masses, you proudly showed me the repairs and redecoration which you have done in your church. "A church must be beautiful," you said. "God and his people must feel at home there."

Your parish lies on the "front lines" — in Flanders' Fields — somewhat hidden between the slopes of a hilly, fertile, agricultural area on the edge of a small woods. Combat was heavy here during the First World War. Not far from your place, next to the Essex Farm Military Cemetery, a plaque was placed on November 15, 1985. It bore the words: "In Flanders' Fields," commemorating the Canadian doctor and officer, John McCrae. His poem of that title was written on May 3, 1915. After my Mission Sunday Sermon, you presented me with this poem, beautifully framed, as a remembrance and a token of friendship.

I came across this text again today when, between conferences, I was leafing through my notes. Rereading the poem, especially the last line, brought me back in thought over space and time to you:

> Take up our quarrel with the foe:
> To you from failing hands we throw
> The torch; be yours to hold it high.
> If you break faith with us who die
> We shall not sleep though poppies grow
> In Flanders' fields.

In an address to your congregation on the day of your appointment, you said: "The land here is sown with the dead bodies of 10,000 young men. But this area is not simply a museum of war or a tourist attraction. The strange consecration that hangs over these fields of slaughter, with their many wartime graves, must be a continual reminder of the things that do not pass away, to the life that is eternal. By our baptism we already share in that life. As your priest I want to help you to preserve it always pure and unadulterated and to share it with one another."

In you, Jos, I have always recognized and respected the man of God — the ordinary priest living among his people, being for them another Christ.

Today I have spoken about Catherine Doherty's Little Mandate to about 100 professed Sisters. Not long ago I gave a talk in your own parish about her life and her contribution in forming a modern day spirituality. You will remember this well. Catherine, of Russian origin and raised in the Byzantine religious world, has had, through her publications and the foundation of Madonna House, a lay apostolic headquarters in Combermere, Ontario, Canada, a tremendous influence on our western Church. Her Little Mandate is

the heart of her message. With the Sisters I reflected on the
words from her Mandate:

> Preach the Gospel WITH YOUR LIFE — WITHOUT COMPROMISE
> — Listen to the Spirit — He will lead you.

Afterwards I sat chatting with Mother Teresa.

"How old are you now?" she asked.

"I'll soon turn 60," I replied.

"A young fellow!" she smiled. "Look at me. I'll be 78,
and I'm still busy for Jesus. How long have you been a
priest?"

"About 35 years. But it took me a long time before I
realized fully what it means to be a priest," I confided to her.
"Do you know, Mother, you — you and Catherine Doherty
have helped me so much to realize anew that Jesus wants to
be a priest in us, and asks us to put at His disposal all that we
have and all that we are. How many years we, His priests, can
leave Him standing before a closed door, despite our belonging, by way of our calling, to the group of His intimate
friends."

"Jesus takes His time, Father," she remarked. "But
sooner or later He comes to possess your heart entirely; to
live in it and to claim you totally for His service. Do you know
what I have been thinking about a lot lately?"

She looked at me and then continued, somewhat shyly,
"On the smallness and humility, the patience of God. He
makes Himself dependent upon us. Jesus is a beggar. He
continually knocks on the door of our hearts and begs to be
let in so that, through us and with us, He can go to the
people. You just said that it took you years before He was
given the chance to fill your whole life with His love. Thirty-
five years really isn't long for Him because His humility
is boundless. God is patient with our weakness and our

sinfulness. You priests must, therefore, also become very small and simple as was Mary the Mother of God in order to become holy as Jesus is holy." She took my breviary, which was beside me, and wrote in it: "Let Jesus through Mary be your whole life."

These words and the talk with Mother Teresa really rejoiced my heart. I want you to share in this happiness, Jos, and that is why I write to you now. A few years ago, when I had celebrated Mass for a group of novices in the little chapel of her house on the Piazza San Gregorio al Celio in Rome, Mother Teresa gave me a book containing thoughts for a priest-collaborator in her Apostolate. On the first page she had written: "Be holy as Jesus is. Be everything for Jesus through Mary. God bless you."

I know that she often inscribes cards and photos and all sorts of books, which she gives as mementos with these words as her message to priests. After my visit to her novitiate in Rome, she gave me the text of a letter she had once written to a priest. Upon arriving home, I translated this letter and distributed it in Flanders. This text I always keep with me, so much has it inspired my priestly life. I now send you a copy of it:

> You have said 'yes' to Jesus and He has taken you at your word. The Word of Jesus became Jesus-poor. And so this terrible emptiness you experience. God cannot fill what is full — He can only fill your emptiness — deep poverty — and your 'yes' is the beginning of your becoming empty. It is not how much we really 'have' to give — but how empty we are — so that we can receive fully in our life and let Him live His life in us.
>
> In you today He wants to relive His complete submission to His Father. Allow Him to do so. It doesn't matter what you feel as long as He feels all right in you. Take away your

eyes from yourself and rejoice that you have nothing. Give Jesus a big smile each time your nothingness frightens you. This is the poverty of Jesus. You and I must let Him live in us and through us in the world.

Cling to Our Lady for she, too, before she could become full of grace, full of Jesus, had to go through that darkness. "How can this be....?" But the moment she said 'yes' she felt a need to go at once, in haste, to give Jesus to John and his family. Keep giving Jesus to your people not by words — but by your example, by being in love with Jesus, by radiating His holiness and spreading His fragrance of Love everywhere you go.

Just keep the joy of Jesus as your strength. Be happy and at peace. Accept whatever He gives and give whatever He takes with a big smile. You belong to Him. Tell Him: "I am Yours, and if You cut me to pieces, every single piece will be only and totally Yours." Let Jesus be the victim and the priest in you. I have started going to visit our houses in India, so I have a beautiful time alone with Jesus on the train.

Pray for me as I do for you.

Yours in Jesus,

M. Teresa, MC

The talk with Mother Teresa about our priesthood brought to mind memories of another great woman of the Church, Catherine Doherty. She also cherished priests in a

very special way. In her book *Dear Father* (originally
published by Alba House, New York, in 1978, and recently
re-issued by Madonna House and available through their
bookstore in Combermere, Ontario), she has penned a message of love to priests and shows her deep respect for them.
The excerpt from this publication that I use here as a basis
for reflection — and did use just recently for a large group
of priests in Calcutta — is exceptionally meaningful. It is
truly a text for meditation:

> We, the laity, call you by the awesome name of "Father"
> because we see you attending to our spiritual needs. Al-
> ways keep in mind that you were ordained to serve us, to
> feed us with the Eucharist, to heal us with anointing, to
> reconcile us to God and to one another in penance, to
> witness our unions of love in marriage and to preach
> God's word.
>
> We, the laity, can be healers in many fashions. We, the
> laity, can be charismatic leaders, doctors, psychologists,
> psychiatrists and social workers. We can even be counsel-
> lors to you, our priests! However, we cannot heal in the
> sacramental sense that you, our priest, can heal. If you
> carry on your own proper healing ministry, you will in-
> spire us, the laity, to carry God's saving Word into the
> inner city and the suburbs, to the rich and the poor. We
> can do all of this as long as you preach the Gospel to us and
> nurture us with the sacraments. We need you present to
> us wherever you may be assigned. We need to be taught by
> your patience, your kindness, your understanding and
> your fortitude, what it is to be a Christian.
>
> Have mercy on us, your ordinary, monotonous, dumpy,
> unleavened flock! Teach us how to love. Teach us to pray.
> Inflame our hearts with the desire to wash the feet of our

poor brethren, to feed them with love, and to preach the Gospel with *our* lives. Send us forth into the world everywhere — the world of poverty, hunger, misery — so that we may change it because we heard your voice 'sending us there' — the Shepherd's voice. Come with us if God appoints you to do so. Lead us wherever He tells us. But do not desert us in order to fulfill personal ambition or your own immediate needs. Always seek to do God's will and you will fulfill your deepest needs and longings.

I gave the text "What is a Priest?" to all of the priests who came to listen to my talk on Catherine Doherty's spirituality. Years ago Catherine's husband, Eddie Doherty, received a letter in which he was asked just what a priest was. He reflected for awhile, but found it difficult to formulate an answer. He went to consult his wife. Without a moment's hesitation, Catherine took a sheet of paper and wrote the following:

A PRIEST is a lover of God,
    a priest is a lover of men,
    a priest is a holy man
        because he walks before the face
        of the All-Holy.

A priest understands all things,
    a priest forgives all things,
    a priest encompasses all things.

The heart of a priest is pierced
    like Christ's
    with the lance of love.

The heart of a priest is open
    like Christ's
    for the whole world to walk through.

The heart of Christ is a vessel of compassion,
    The heart of a priest is a chalice
        of love.

The heart of a priest is a trysting place
    of human and divine love.

A priest is a man who has crucified himself
    so that he, too, may be lifted up
    and draw all things to Christ.

A priest is a man in love with God.

A priest is the symbol of the Word made flesh;
    a priest is the naked sword of God's justice;
    a priest is the hand of God's mercy;
    a priest is the reflection of God's love.

    Nothing can be greater in this world
    than a priest; nothing but God himself!

Is it not striking, dear Jos, that both of these prominent and saintly women should remind us that we must be true and holy priests?

Before the exposition of the Blessed Sacrament and the evening prayers, the Sisters brought me a cup of coffee, and Mother Teresa came to chat awhile in the small sacristy of the chapel on the first floor. She told me that she had just sent a letter to all the bishops of the world to let them know of the affection and concern all the Missionaries of Charity have for priests. I am sending you the contents of this letter just as I received it from her. It is news "hot off the press."

Missionaries of Charity
54 A., Lower Circular Road
December 14, 1987

Your Grace,

To satiate the thirst of Jesus on the Cross for you and for
each of your priests in your beloved diocese, I would love
to offer each of you a Sister, individually, who will offer all
she is and has to Jesus through Mary, the Mother of the
Church, for you or for the priest whom you give to her in
spiritual, missionary adoption, like St. Therese of Lisieux
had done, so that Jesus who is in agony in His priests,
scourged in His priests, may find a Veronica to help Him
on His way to Calvary, so that He may be able to rise with
the splendor of His Resurrection in His priests and thus
bring about a new Pentecost not only in your diocese, but
in the whole Church.

So, please send me the names of all the priests in your
diocese as soon as possible, as a sign of your acceptance of
this my offering.

Please keep me and all of us in your prayers and in the
Eucharistic Sacrifice.

God bless you!

M. Teresa, MC

When I had read this letter, Mother Teresa smiled
radiantly and said: "Do you know, Father, what the Holy
Father said to me when he gave his permission to send this
letter to all the bishops? 'I want to be the first priest to be
adopted by one of your Sisters. Even the Pope needs your
prayers and sacrifices!' "

She gave me a white card with the name of a Sister on it, and the words: "I, Sister Maria Ricta, offer all that I am and have to Jesus through Mary, Our Mother, for you, Father Omer. Calcutta, December 4, 1987." We remained sitting awhile, and Mother Teresa continued: "Whenever you come in contact with my Sisters in any part of the world, you must give them the Eucharist before anything else. Bless them with this Most Holy Sacrament. Take the time to be available so that they can receive the Sacrament of Penance and Reconciliation. Without you priests, it is impossible for us to be good Missionaries of Charity."

In their houses in Europe, India and Canada, I was always struck by a sign hanging on the sacristy wall. Clearly it was intended for the visiting priest: "Celebrate the Holy Mass as if it were your first, your last, or the only one of your whole life." What I heard today, dear Jos, in the little sacristy of the Motherhouse in Calcutta, during my chats with Mother Teresa about our priesthood, helps me to understand more clearly than ever the words in Catherine Doherty's Little Mandate:

Preach the Gospel WITH YOUR LIFE — WITHOUT COMPROMISE — Listen to the Spirit — He will lead you.

It is the Spirit who leads us in the words He has given to these remarkable women and in the witness of their lives. He will help us so that our priestly lives will continually point to Jesus and His Gospel. It was with the greatest respect for Jesus, the Priest, in us that Catherine Doherty said to me every time that I met her in Madonna House and when I asked her for a cross at my departure: "I do not bless you. You were ordained to bless us and make us holy through the Triune God living in you — the Father, the Son, and the Holy Spirit. Give me your priestly blessing. Then I will place on your head the icon I received from my holy mother when I had to flee Russia in 1917. And I will ask the *Theotokos*, the Mother of God, to make you a holy priest."

This has become a long letter, dear Jos, but it is one which I have actually written for myself as well as you. Fr. Roger Vandersteene, our mutual friend, was a missionary for thirty years among the Cree Indians, in the forests of the Canadian Far North. Until his death in 1976, he was an exceptional priest. I still recall his words during his last holiday in Flanders: "It is rather surprising that you priests all speak about so very many things, but so seldom mention the One who fills our lives — Jesus! We should speak more about Him and about our joy in being able to live and die as His priests."

That is why I wanted to write this heart-to-heart letter to you. In the past days I have had many contacts with priests and missionaries. I had the occasion to share Catherine Doherty's love and concern for priests with them. Catherine of Combermere, or Catherine of the Cross as they called her after her death, called me and each priest of the Madonna House Apostolate her priest sons.

We held an hour of adoration with the archbishop and prayed for all of the priests in the world. I included you and each of our brother priests in our diocese. Let us pray to Jesus for one another, dear Jos, so that the words "To you we throw the torch; be yours to hold it high," as we read in John McCrae's poem, may be true of you with your people in Flanders' Fields, and of me here with the priests and the Missionary Sisters of Charity in Calcutta, the city of joy and the city of saints. May we truly hold high that torch.

I greet you warmly, grateful for your affection and faithful friendship.

Omer

LETTER III:
POVERTY IS OUR DOWRY

To the Missionaries of Charity in Ghent

Calcutta, December 6, 1987

Dear Sisters,

I have written most of this letter in the little sacristy of your Motherhouse on Lower Circular Road. The room serves as guest quarters during the course of the days of recollection I am giving here. It contains a confessional, a large cupboard for the vestments and church linen, a table and chair. You can hardly move about in it, but it is very peaceful — a welcome respite from the noise of the city.

A few days before my departure, we prepared together for my visit during the celebration of the Eucharist and the ensuing time of adoration there in your simple, little house in the Beginjnengracht in Ghent. During these days which I am spending with your Sisters in Calcutta, you have been interceding for us, especially in silence and in prayer, that Jesus, in the silence and prayer of these days of recollection, would grow ever more in me and fill me and your Sisters with His presence and His love. For this, I am truly grateful.

Two things caught my attention this morning when I entered your house: In order to reach the first floor, where the large chapel with its small, adjacent sacristy is located, you have to pass through the corridor close to the entrance and then go through the courtyard with its grotto to Our Lady before climbing the stone stairs which lead to the chapel and your private quarters.

The first thing I noticed was the silver and white bucket of one of your Sisters, with its number "1,391." This same number appears on your white and blue saris and other articles of clothing. It indicates the numerical order of your entry into the Community.

On the inner balcony of the first floor, the second thing that struck me was the small prayer-clock with the monthly prayer intention under it: "For the evangelization of Europe." You have a very personal contribution to make in this evangelization. It flows from the spirituality and mission of your Congregation. During the opening ceremonies of the first foundation of the Missionaries of Charity in Belgium in Ghent, on June 1, 1988, Mother Teresa told the large gathering assembled in the church of the Carmelites: "We have come to Flanders to witness to God's love for mankind in his poor. Your missionaries have brought Jesus and His Gospel to India. They are still there, and they will remain with us until their deaths. The Church of India is grateful. Now it is her turn to send missionaries here because in your land, also, there are people hungry for affection and for God. Let us pray fervently that we will learn to see our own poverty and that of others."

Regularly we pray for this here with your fellow Sisters. Today we dedicated a long period of meditation to the words given to Catherine Doherty in her Little Mandate:

Sell all you possess. . . .
Give it directly, personally to the poor — being poor —
being one with them — one with Me.

What she taught her followers about poverty is completely in accord with your own vocation and mission as Missionaries of Charity, and to us in Europe as well.

"Poverty is our dowry," Mother Teresa wrote in the Introduction to Chapter 7 of your Constitutions. Reading this chapter, I have seen that Mother Teresa's and Catherine Doherty's ideas on poverty have the same characteristics. It is clear that both women considered material and spiritual poverty as essential in the lives of those who desire to follow Jesus and bring His love to the poor. The fact that there are religious and lay people who choose to experience material poverty in a radical way as evangelical witnesses is a constant source of amazement and admiration to both believers and unbelievers alike.

Not long ago, a missionary from India, who was home in Flanders on leave, said to me: "The Sisters of Mother Teresa whom I saw at work in Ranchi and Calcutta are extremely conscientious religious. The poor way in which they live is simply staggering." The simplicity of your housing, clothing and way of life attracts more people than you will ever realize. Common dormitories, simple furnishings, the absence of all sorts of modern appliances such as radio or television — all these are discreet but telling signs of the poverty in which you have chosen to live. The desire to live in this close solidarity with the materially poor is a witness to the sincerity of your dedication.

I remember two years ago when we all sat talking before Mother Teresa's departure for Rome, after her visit to Flanders. We were in the palace in Laken. The King entered the parlor with the Queen and Mother Teresa and, obviously still moved by the conversation that he and the Queen had had with Mother Teresa, he whispered to me: "Father, this woman is filled with God." He then asked Mother Teresa what he could offer her to drink. "Thank you," she replied very politely, "but no. We never accept anything to eat or drink when we visit. The poor in their hovels and slums are seldom offered anything, so out of respect and empathy for them, we, too, always refuse. I hope you'll understand."

I could observe, during my stay in Calcutta, that you live an unconditional poverty. The bucket with its number, the dinner utensils, the wooden beds, the hard benches and chairs, and your total dependence on donations make it more than clear that you want to live with a blind faith in God's Providence. It is written in your Constitutions:

> Since we and our poor will depend entirely on Divine Providence both for our material and spiritual needs,
>
> a) we will first allow ourselves to be God's Providence to His people by seeking first His kingdom and His right-eousness, by laboring wholeheartedly to bring God into their lives.

I have also experienced this blind trust in God's care for each of us in Madonna House at Combermere. "How do you live?" I asked one of the staff members.

"Why, we entrust ourselves to Divine Providence," she replied.

There, in Madonna House, poverty is also lived in a radical kind of way. On Friday evenings everyone fasts, and many keep individual fasts on other days as well. Meat is usually eaten only on Sundays. Meals are prepared frugally from what the farm produces. All of the staff wear second-hand clothing. Household articles are gifts of benefactors. I have told you many times, during our days of recollection, how much you have in common with what Catherine Doherty and the dedicated members of her community witness to by their way of life.

I was deeply impressed one time when Mother Teresa arrived at the Belgian National Airport in Zaventem. She had been in Rome and the only baggage she carried was a small handbag and a cardboard box which served as a suitcase. Written in bold letters on the brown box, fastened only with a cord, was: "Mother Teresa." In her bag, along with her passport and plane ticket, she had stashed away in a plastic container the breakfast that had been served on the plane. "I took that with me to give to the poor," she said laughingly. "You mustn't waste anything." It made me think of that 15th of October in 1938 when Catherine Doherty went to live in the slums of Toronto. After having given away all that she possessed, she went to live in a cheap, dirty, smelly room in a poor section of the city. The clothes that she wore, a small suitcase, a change of underclothes was all that she took. It was from their direct contact with the concrete reality of the poorest of the poor — there in Toronto and here in Calcutta — that these two holy women were inspired to live and powerfully develop the spirituality that they have since passed on to us.

On my first visit to Calcutta, twenty years ago now, I had a long discussion with Mother Teresa about the problems of development and the need to search out and eradicate the very roots of poverty and injustice. She agreed that this was, indeed, very important, but that in the meantime you couldn't ignore the immediate needs of the poor:

"I don't desire that you give from your abundance. I want you to understand through direct contact. By our work with the poorest of the poor we touch Jesus at every moment of the day and night. The poor need deeds, not words. It is not my task to evaluate existing systems, economic, social, or political structures and ideologies. Everyone has a conscience and must follow it. How often I have been told that I mustn't give the hungry fish, but rather gear with which to fish! My God, usually they don't even have the strength to hold a rod! If I do give them fish, at least I give them the strength so that, perhaps, they can go fishing tomorrow.

"There are people in this world who do fight for justice and human rights, and who do their best to change dis-criminating structures. We don't want to ignore that, but our mission consists in approaching the problems individu-ally rather than collectively. We look for the people with whom Jesus Christ identified when He said: 'I was hungry,' 'I was sick. . . .' We will come to understand the problems of poverty not only by reading about them, but by going into the slums full of admiration for all that is being done there. We have to enter into poverty itself, to share it, to experience it together."

My friend and confrere, Francois Laborde, who works in the Pilkana slums, told a German journalist who visited him in his little house in Howrah, "It's easy for everyone to recognize and value the riches of the world, but only the poor know the richness that suffering brings." Not long ago, in a Dutch missionary magazine, I read the witness of Bishop Labayen from the Philippines: "In the past we drew our spirituality from different sources. We drew it from contemplatives, priests and religious as, for example, little Therese of Lisieux. Today we will find it by sitting at the feet of the poor."

There it is again. How striking it is how this "at the feet of the poor" developed in the Nazareth spirituality of Catherine Doherty and the "I Thirst" spirituality of Mother

Teresa. Both hold up for their followers a very special evangelical experience of God's love for all people everywhere. Through all the humble, everyday work carried out in the slums, the encounter with God in the poorest of the poor still remains central.

Do you recall, dear Sisters, how several months ago, during a day of recollection, we discussed several chapters from your Constitutions? I chose a specific text for you from your rules, and today I read it again during one of my conferences for your Sisters here. It tells us that Christ calls us through His Church to love Him freely and with our whole heart in our consecrated lives in the service of the poorest of the poor. He identified Himself with these poor. He is present in them in order to become known, loved and served by all; in order that reparation might be made for the sins of hate, indifference and lack of love. This calling that comes from the Heart of Jesus to serve Him unconditionally and to love Him in His pitiful disguise in the poor is our personal vocation in the Church today.

This vocation supposes a true service to the poorest of the poor by feeding the hungry not only with food, but also with the Word of God; by giving the thirsty not only water to drink, but also knowledge, truth, peace, justice and love; by clothing the naked not only with garments, but also with human dignity; by giving the homeless shelter not only by finding them homes, but also by showing them a heart that understands them, that protects them, that loves them; by caring for the sick and the dying and by attending to them not only physically, but also spiritually; by announcing the Gospel to them through our presence and our works of charity.

You know that Mother Teresa also often spoke about the spiritually poor who must find a generous place in the Heart of Jesus and in our own. These poor you find everywhere because "Calcutta is everywhere." The deepest poverty is that which is hidden in one's own heart. You may not reduce it to the simple absence of material things necessary for survival.

Following a visit to India, a friend of mine spoke about what he called the "pornography of hunger." By that he referred to those who harbor an almost sickly curiosity about those who live in crowded slums and in those who simply lie there dying.

Catherine Doherty also spoke of this when she wrote in her book *The Gospel Without Compromise* (Ave Maria Press, Notre Dame, Indiana, 1976):

> It seems to me that everybody in the Catholic world is suddenly rushing to the poor. Everybody is boarding a bus, train, or plane to go and do something for the poor and the downtrodden. These "invisible ones" have been with us for a long time. Now they become the newly discovered land to which all must go and *do* something.

> No one seems to want to begin at the beginning! The beginning, of course, is ourselves, each one of us. *We are the unknown land.*

> Christ said, "Love your neighbor as yourself." Who is this self that God wants us to love first, before we try to love anyone else? Am I not the poorest of all? Would I take a bus, train, or plane to discover my own poverty, my own need of God?

> . . . The crisis of today is not exactly the poor, though they are part of it. *The crisis of today is man himself.* This exodus, this flight from oneself into feverish activity, is often a flight, an escape from meeting oneself. Living in the slums and offering our manifold competencies to the poor is not the answer — or should I say is not the answer,

not the first answer. Others also — communists, humanitarians of all kinds — have many of the same competencies we have, and often in greater depth.

. . . I know what it means to be poor, destitute, cold, hungry and alone. I've spent thirty-six years of my life in the rural and city slums of Canada. But did I have the right to go to those tenements to the poor, to seek Christ in those hovels and alleyways before I found Him in the manger of my own heart?

. . . The crisis of today is the crisis of faith. It isn't in the liturgy; it isn't social justice; it isn't the poor. It is faith. Without faith we cannot love ourselves, cannot see the image of God in our hearts. The crib of our own hearts is empty of God. If we do not see Him in ourselves, we will not be able to see Him in others.

Only then can the Christ in us meet the Christ in the other. Then, and only then, can we go to the poor to feed them both the bread they need to live, and the bread of justice, their restored dignity as human beings. But above all, we must give them the bread and the wine of Christ's body, His living words of truth. In a word, we must bring them Christ for whom they hunger without even knowing it.

Yes, before we kneel before the Christ in hovels and broken down tenement buildings, we must be able to kneel before the Christ of our hearts. Is He there? This is the question, and it concerns the very essence of poverty. Are we actually seeking to run away from our own poverty, the crisis of faith within ourselves, and escape into the lulling, consoling, emotionally satisfying world of the poor? . . . It is in this *poustinia* of our own hearts that we will experience Jesus.

"The more the image of God in the poor is disfigured, the greater our faith and our dedication in seeking the face of Jesus must be," Mother Teresa tells us. Is this not your greatest challenge, dear Sisters, as Missionaries of Charity? As religious who have chosen a life of poverty in the service of the poorest of the poor? You know that these poor are not only the people of Calcutta or the many areas of misery and starvation in the Southern Hemisphere, or the handicapped, the unborn or the destitute of the industrialized world. They are also the numerous lonely and embittered people whom we meet daily on the street, on buses or trains, in department stores, in hospitals, in homes for the aged, in flats and high class living rooms. Often people with power and respect, with money and possessions are unhappy because they lack love and tenderness.

During our retreat in your house there in Ghent, three years ago, Mother Teresa told me how shocked she was by the spiritual poverty that she sees in the crowded row houses, the tenement flats and the residential areas of our large cities. "People live here who are poorer still than the slum residents of Calcutta," she remarked. "They have a crying need for Jesus. They belong to the poorest of the poor. We must visit them with the Heart of Jesus and give it to them."

Daily in your houses in Europe and North America you receive the down-and-out, the rejects of society, the refugees from our so-called Third World, and you give them food and clothing and shelter. You go to visit them in the hospitals where they end up in one of the wards provided for them by the social services of the community. But others who suffer from wounded hearts knock on your doors as well — persons whose hearts are in desperate need of love and understanding; people who are looking for Jesus. To all of these poor you are able to offer the richness of your inner poverty and the purity and the emptiness of a heart in which God has His dwelling.

The words from the Little Mandate of Catherine Doherty which we meditated upon today were:

> Sell all you possess. . . . Give it directly, personally to the poor. Take up My cross (their cross) and follow Me — going to the poor — being poor — being one with them — one with Me.

Becoming poor means for you, as for all of our Madonna House members, dispossessing yourselves of everything, externally and internally, begging for your own physical needs and those of the destitute; going to live in their midst, so that they, ultimately, will realize the poverty of the cross.

Mother Teresa said: "When Our Lord asked His religious Sisters to carry on their work among the poor, He then explicitly asked them to accept the poverty of the cross. He chose poverty because this is the means of possessing God and of bringing His love to the people. God desires our littleness and our emptiness — not our fullness."

A saying of Mother Teresa hangs in the small refectory of your house in the Beginjnengracht, where guests who come to ask for food or help are welcomed daily between 5 a.m. and 6 p.m. Every time I come to celebrate the Eucharist with you, it strikes me anew. "I will present saints to Our Mother, the Holy Church." Saints of poverty; saints who sit at the feet of the poor. This striving towards holiness through the poverty of the cross, dear Sisters, will be your dowry for Jesus. In this poverty you are bound and united to Him forever.

The words that Catherine Doherty once wrote to a few Madonna House staff members, who were preparing to make their final promises, apply also to you. They are the last lines of her poetic description of her union with the Crucified Jesus on the day that she went to live amidst the poor in the slums of Toronto.

> Yes, I would not exchange my wedding day to God, in that gray, shabby room, on that gray October day, for any day anywhere! (*Journey Inward*, Alba House, N.Y., 1984)

For our reflection during our time of worship, I read a few more fragments from the Madonna House Constitutions. They are words that can also serve for you:

> Your road is long, your road is dusty. You will be living in the alleys and byways of the world. Yours is the stinking backyards. Yours are the places nobody wants to go to. Yours are the immense stretches of desert that exist in men's souls. You will have to cross the seas of despair and doubt in their hearts. Can you take any baggage on this strange journey? No! And so to your obedience and love is added poverty. . . .

> . . . Our vocation is simple, so utterly simple that words fail to describe it. It is intangible and yet very concrete. To burn. To do the will of God in the humble duty of every moment. To die to self through obedience, poverty, and love. Through chastity too: to have no one who belongs to you, and your belonging to no one, except God. To live in the present moment. To be ready to be crucified (in the mystical sense) on the cross of the will of God. To be ready to be crucified by men. You will be. You will be crucified with their words, not yet realizing that words spoken by men are like chaff in the wind. . . .

I must prove to My Beloved that I love Him. Words are not enough! Words die before the Word. I can only prove my love for Him by loving my neighbor, for my neighbor is He Himself.

Leaving the small, peaceful sacristy, I went to sit awhile in the chapel that looks out over the street. Again I was taken up into the screaming noise of Calcutta. The windows were open; the piercing cry of crows, cars honking unceasingly, talking, laughing, shouting voices all gushed inside.

"Jesus," I prayed, "bless the Sisters here and those in my own country who so desire to become holy, in the heart of the city, for the poorest of Your poor."

Within a few weeks, at the end of this year, I hope to be with you again to celebrate the Eucharist with you and to spend New Year's Eve with you in worship. I greet you all from Mother Teresa's house here — a house that is also yours.

With my priestly blessings,

Fr. Omer

LETTER IV:

SOMETHING BEAUTIFUL FOR GOD

To Geert and Willem, Foster Parents

Calcutta, December 9, 1987

Dear Friends,

Nirmala Shishu Bhavan is the home for abandoned children on Lower Circular Road. Mother Teresa took it over in 1952, calling it the *Children's Home of the Immaculate Virgin.* After having opened that year the Nirmal Hriday for the dying who had been abandoned, it seemed only natural that a place for the care of abandoned children should follow. The three Indian children who are now a part of your own family, Geert and Willem, were taken in here, cared for, and gotten ready for their eventual foster parents.

Very early this morning two Sisters from the Nirmala community came to get me at the archbishop's residence where I am staying. Yesterday, Sister Shanti, their superior, had asked me to celebrate the Eucharist for them and then give a conference about Catherine Doherty's spirituality.

It is an exciting experience to walk through the streets of Calcutta in the early morning hours. A huge slumbering city is awakening. One could already spot life in many places along the sidewalks, for it is there under the gunnysack tents that the poor of the city live. A few sat huddled in a sort of blanket, silently warming themselves by a smouldering fire. I thought about what one of my companions had said to me as he accompanied me back to the archbishop's home on Park Street. It was after a gathering of lay leaders from the various parishes of the city. We had had a good meeting and there, too, we had discussed the lay spirituality of Madonna House in Combermere. As I stepped onto the sidewalk, my companion said to me: "No. In Calcutta you must walk in the streets in the evening. The sidewalk is for the poor. That is their domain. Leave it to them."

There was already much hustle and bustle in and around St. Xavier's University College on Park Street. Morning courses were already under way. Taxis and rickshaws delivered their clients and then drove off discreetly as if they didn't want to violate the quiet of the morning.

All about the vicinity of the Maidan — an open square measuring a good three and a half kilometers (approx. 2 miles) in the very heart of the city close to Chowringhee, Fort William, the Victoria Memorial and the Governor's House (an area once redeemed from the jungle) — one sees scores of people, some just strolling about and others doing Yoga exercises. The Sisters who accompanied me were silent. They, too, were a part of this great world on the verge of awakening — one that, within a few hours, would be transformed once more into a noisy, bustling, nerve-racking city. The Sisters fingered their rosaries as they led me to the chapel on the first floor of Shishu Bhavan.

After Mass we had breakfast with the Sisters. During it I heard a group of older children with their monitors singing their morning prayers before the statue of Our Lady in the courtyard. It is here that you often see trucks and ambulances arriving with loads of clothing, food and medicine from our own country. In the same courtyard, about ten years ago, I saw a German television crew making a documentary on Mother Teresa and her work. The following year it was televised on New Year's Eve immediately prior to a tasteless entertainment program.

I can still recall ever so clearly the talk I had with Mother Teresa between the filming sessions. It was about the vocation crisis in Europe. With terms discreetly adapted to the occasion and in phrases that were carefully honed, I spoke somewhat pompously about the probable causes for the very dramatic decline in vocations. I mentioned secularization, the changing image of the Church and the crisis of faith that was apparent everywhere in our materialistically minded western culture. Mother Teresa listened for a moment and then interrupted. "Father, all of you back there in Europe talk too much and put on too many airs. You would be better to talk more about Jesus."

Every time I come to this house, I experience how one understands the Gospel so much better when one looks at those who witness to it in every fiber of their being, in every action that they perform. Everything in this Home for Abandoned Children points to the God who abandons no one.

Sister Shanti, a medical doctor and one of Mother Teresa's closest helpers, invited me to greet the children and the nursing staff. In the small vestibule of the children's pavilion, I noticed a colorful poster depicting a child with a bright and smiling face. On it were the words: "Something beautiful for God!"

As soon as they spotted us, a number of the children came running up, wanting to be picked up and caressed.

"Give them a Sign of the Cross, Father," Sister suggested. "In a few days' time, some of them will be leaving here for foster parents in your own land." At this, I immediately thought about the two of you with your three darling children now already grown into healthy, fine young people.

The Home here is full of babies and little children. An Indian woman who frequently offers her services in Shishu Bhavan came to show Sister Shanti an unbelievably small baby resting in the palm of her hand. "This was an aborted child," Sister remarked. "It's doing fine now, though, and will survive. Won't you give it your blessing, Father, please?"

Seeing all the adorable faces of the youngsters here, many of whom have been brought here sick, abandoned, or starving, moved me deeply. How did Sartre put it? "L'enfant, c'est un chose vomie." "A child is vomit, something entirely superfluous." But here they are taken in as if they were the Child of Bethlehem Himself, pursued, persecuted, and put to death by the selfishness of adults. "Unborn children belong to the poorest of the poor," Mother Teresa says. Whoever commits abortion prevents these little ones from loving and being loved, just as God loves us. Everything here points to love and simplicity. It struck me that all those who work and want to care for and love these children as the Child Jesus Himself, also treat *me* as a priest. "Bless them, Father, please. Let them feel that Jesus in you loves them all, because they are poor and small and childlike," Sister Shanti had said to me.

I wrote, dear Geert and Willem, that I was invited here to give a conference for about 30 novices and 20 professed Sisters who work in Shishu Bhavan. For my talks I have chosen a fragment from Catherine Doherty's Little Mandate:

Little — be always little . . . simple — poor — childlike.

This is one of the fundamentals of the spiritual life as you so often hear it described by both Catherine and Mother Teresa. In a Staff Letter of May 30, 1959, Catherine Doherty wrote to her followers:

> The Spirit of Madonna House Institute is one of childlike simplicity. To be childlike and simple means not to evade Calvary. Childlike simplicity faces the very simple fact that there is no evading the cross, and being crucified on it and dying to self. For only thus can we love Him back.
>
> So away with all the tortuous arguments! We are walking from where we are now to that cross, without deviating from that direct path. That is what is meant by childlike simplicity in its most fundamental and simple form.

And in a Christmas letter for 1976, she wrote:

> When we reach Bethlehem, our heart will fall and adore Him quite naturally. We will understand, while we stand there, how the creche, made of wood, blends with the cross which has also been made of wood. And, in standing before the Child in that creche (that will change in shape in time to come), we will understand that this is our life too. We, too, are in a creche; we, too, are really journeying to a cross; we, too, follow in His footsteps.
>
> And so, my dearly beloved, it might not be a long Christmas letter, but it comes to you from my heart. I shall journey with you to Bethlehem. Today, we shall walk on the journey from Bethlehem to Golgotha. Together we shall know once again (although we already know it) that we live in the resurrected Christ.

Catherine Doherty had a great devotion to the Child Jesus. God becoming man as a small, defenseless child was the greatest revelation of His own self-emptying for the love of us that He could have ever made.

One of the prayers Catherine especially loved appears on a plaque which bears a sculpture of the Child Jesus in swaddling clothes. It is mounted on one of the walls of the wooden chapel at Madonna House in Combermere, the Training Center for her Lay Apostolate. It is: "Give me the heart of a child and the awesome courage to live it out."

Bethlehem, the Slaughter of the Innocents, and the indescribable suffering of so many children in this world are easily understood in Shishu Bhavan. In the book of Catherine's interior conversations, *Journey Inward* (Alba House, 1984), we find:

Child in Pain, Christmas 1972

Suddenly Bethlehem was in our midst — in the alley with the garbage, in the hospital of abortion, in the foundling wrapped in red tape.

Yes, suddenly Bethlehem — manger and cave — were here. And You came with them.

It was here in the upper room of Shishu Bhavan that I came with Mother Teresa on an afternoon in July 1968. We came to see a baby that she had found that very morning in one of the slums. The baby lay in a crib; it had an ashen color and was receiving blood plasma and serum. In my mind I still clearly see how Mother Teresa took the child in her large, rough hands and gently stroked its face. "My little brother," she whispered.

"What do you mean, Mother?" I asked.

She looked at me, dismayed by my somewhat affected question, and placed the child before me. "Look, Father. Look at this child. God lives in him because He loves him, just as He loves all people — especially the poor, especially the little. That's why He wants to live in them just as He lives in you and me. When God abides in us and lives His life in and through us, we are eternal. We die no longer. We become godly people. In God we are one another's brothers and sisters. I have become a missionary in order to show and proclaim this to people here in India where most neither know nor realize this. You, Father, must do so in Europe where so many seem to have forgotten it."

Again she stroked the baby's face. She is caressing God, I thought, and recalled a story Catherine Doherty once told me: "When I was a child," she said, "my good mother often spoke to me about God. One day I asked her, 'But, Mama, you never stop talking about God who is so concerned about me and loves me so very much. I would like, just once, to see this God with my own eyes and to touch Him. How can we arrange this?' 'By touching me, my child,' she answered."

When — on that July day I was telling you about earlier — Mother Teresa and I were leaving the room where the sick and premature babies were being cared for, a few older children came running up to us as they did this morning with Sister Shanti. Mother Teresa took them in her arms and hugged them. "Bless them, Father," she said. I laid my hands on them all and signed their foreheads with a cross, just as you do with your three Indian children, Geert and Willem, before they go to sleep, or when they come to say good morning to you in your bedroom.

How often I have thought of them in Shishu Bhavan. Of Sushi with her beautiful, long black hair and laughing eyes, who was entrusted to Mother Teresa's care as the only surviving member of her family following a flood. Of Jo, your son, who was discovered by a catechist somewhere in the undergrowth of the Orissa jungle and brought here. Of Anand, your youngest daughter with her giggly voice, who can speak the sing-song dialect of your region so beautifully, and who has such a keen mind. She was abandoned among the garbage heaps of the Pilkana slums in Calcutta. Passersby who heard her cries brought her to Shishu Bhavan. You have adopted all three, cared for them, and brought them up.

"I give children to families, not because we can't care for them ourselves, but in order that they may know the tender love of a mother and a father," Mother Teresa said during her meeting with the "Sowers of Joy," as all of you foster parents of Indian children are called. You both heard her address to those more than a thousand foster parents and their adopted children there in Flanders in October of 1986. As you will recall, she emphasized at the time our oneness with Jesus.

"This is exactly what Jesus wants to teach us. To love one another as He loves us. And where does this love begin? In our own family; in our own community; in our own parish. And how does it begin? By praying together. A family, a community, a parish that prays together, stays together. If we stay together, then we will love one another as God loves us. That's why it is so important in a family to teach the children to pray and to pray with them. If we don't do this, it will be difficult to carry on and to become holy because the fruit of prayer is a deepening of our faith. The fruit of faith is love; the fruit of love is service; the fruit of service is peace. All this is the consequence of our oneness with Christ, when we allow Him to pray in and with us."

Your adopted children, Geert and Willem, are happy children. You know that Jesus is present in them. Whenever

I come to your home, I see that love and a spirit of service and joy pervade everything because you pray together with them. Hundreds of parents in our country are doing the same thing with other children. Children from Africa, Korea, Vietnam, or Belgium itself, who, for one reason or another, were abandoned to their fate, or who never knew the love of a real father or mother. I can just imagine what this demands in regard to care and adaptation.

On more than one occasion, as I returned to Belgium with groups who had visited India, we brought back with us children who had been entrusted to us by the Sisters in Calcutta or Bombay. They were destined for adoption. During the long trip, it was delightful to see how they gradually became accustomed to us. One by one they crawled onto our laps, romped and played with us. I saw their little faces and those of the foster parents waiting for them in the entrance hall of the airport.

What moving scenes I have experienced! I've seen how these good people, who had waited so long to hug a child — their own child — took these Indian orphans and abandoned children passionately in their arms. Often the children themselves, completely taken aback and confused, didn't actually realize what was happening to them. You must know, Geert and Willem, that, whenever I see Sushi, Jo, and Anand, your children and hear them speaking and listening in their own language, I can't help but think of Shishu Bhavan.

"Make something beautiful of your lives. . . ." I have seen so many people who visit this Children's Home cry, people who were visiting Calcutta and wanted to see the "famous Mother Teresa" and her houses and works. This seems to belong to the list of things people consider worthwhile doing in this city. These are simple, ordinary people as well as sophisticated intellectuals. There are journalists and tourists — people traveling in search of answers to their many questions about life.

Only a few are able to resist the helplessness and the smiles of these children. Here one has to become very small and childlike. Here one learns to see the Christ Child. Is this not one of life's biggest challenges — to become as Jesus, the most perfect Child of the Father? Childlikeness is, for a Christian, no free choice. It is not simply one spirituality among others. Jesus has told us that *unless* we become as little children, we cannot enter the kingdom of heaven. I believe that it is biblically justified to claim that one of the most imperative tasks in our lives is no less than an ongoing exploration of who we are created to be — children of our heavenly Father.

When I took leave of Sister Shanti in the Children's Home, she asked me to pray "that we may always preserve untarnished the charism of our Congregation."

The care of the poorest of the poor in these abandoned children reminds us of this charism: to become as unimportant and unpretentious as these children so that Jesus can grow in us. Do you remember, Geert and Willem, how Mother Teresa attacked the problem of abortion during her visit to Flanders? She referred to the Gospel story about Mary, hurrying to Elizabeth to share the good news that Jesus was with her. Elizabeth, too, was pregnant, and the child in her leapt with joy on Mary's arrival. "It is strange," Mother Teresa said, "that God chose an unborn child to announce the coming of Christ!" But, if we are to understand and accept the coming and the presence of God-made-man in us, we must become as little children.

We live in a time of such great religious women as Mother Teresa and Catherine Doherty, both well known in the world and in the Church. Popularity and success can sometimes lead one to exaggerate one's self-importance and to think that God has called one to continue His work precisely because one is so great. To think like this is to forget that it is really only a humble acceptance of one's vocation that can make one great.

Many times Catherine Doherty repeated to her spiritual family these words taken from her Staff Letter of December 17, 1958:

> Let us be content to be misunderstood. Let us be content to be maligned, to be "made little of." For aren't we small, if not in numbers (though we are that yet), then in importance? And let us not worry about it. For the Lord was small in Bethlehem, and those who are small in Him will someday be BIG before His face — but not now. Yes, let us be small, humble, poor . . . ready to live with what we have . . . making our home in Bethlehem and Nazareth, now and forever.

Mother Teresa also realized that she should be the last and the least of all children. She is convinced that God chose her to astound the world because of her exceptional love for Jesus in the least privileged and the smallest of this world. That's why she constantly repeats: "We do it for Jesus."

When I once tried to rescue her from a swarm of photographers and journalists, during one of her visits to Belgium, she laughingly said: "Let them alone, Father. It is, after all, for Jesus," and she immediately hurried over to a handicapped child who was shouting for all he was worth from his wheelchair. She kissed his forehead, and pressed him lovingly to her heart.

She once told me about Malcolm Muggeridge who, as a searching agnostic, wrote one of the first biographies about her, *Something Beautiful for God* (William Collins Sons and Co., Ltd., London, 1971). Mother Teresa said to me: "I can still see him crying his heart out in the chapel of our Motherhouse following his first visit to Nirmal Hriday and Shishu Bhavan. I went to him and said, 'Malcolm, one day I'm going to be present at your First Communion.' And I was. Beautiful things do happen for God!"

In your lives, too, dear Geert and Willem, beautiful things happen because you have given love to children. Both of you, along with many other foster parents around the world, realize that what you do daily for your adopted children is also something beautiful for God. Through these little ones, God also helps us to become simple and childlike ourselves.

During the Mass this morning in Nirmala Shishu Bhavan, I prayed for all the foster parents of "Sowers of Joy," together with the 50 Missionaries of Charity who were present there. After Mass they sang one of their most beautiful hymns:

> "Show each one something beautiful for God above
> Something beautiful to show your love. . . ."

I now say "Good-bye" from the Children's Home in Calcutta. Kiss Sushi, Jo, and Anand for me. And sign their foreheads with the Sign of the Cross.

Much love,

Omer

LETTER V:
WHERE IS JESUS?

To Archbishop Joseph

Calcutta, December 12, 1987

Bishop, My dear Brother in Jesus,

The residence of Archbishop Henry D'Souza here is a tall, imposing building dating from the British Colonial Period. Money raised by mission-minded people in our Belgian city of Antwerp helped to fund it as one can read on a white memorial stone on the first floor.

Calcutta's first archbishop was Bishop Paul Goethals of West Flanders who directed the then Apostolic Vicariate of West Bengal from 1886-1891. Fr. Brice Muelmans, S.J., succeeded him as bishop until 1924. Then came Archbishop Ferdinand Perier, S.J., of Antwerp. It was he who, in 1958, was to encourage and support Mother Teresa in forging and working out her new Congregation, the Missionaries of Charity. He was followed by Cardinal Laurence Pichachi, S.J., and, in 1986, Henry D'Souza succeeded him.

In 1974, the year that he was consecrated bishop, D'Souza's mother died. Mother Teresa came to visit him and said, "Bishop, now you need another mother to care for you. I will be your mother from now on." On the day of his consecration, Bishop Henry told me, the ceremony was well under way when in walked Mother Teresa. She went straight to the first pew, sat down next to his father, and looked Henry straight in the eye, as if to say, "See, I did come! I am here, and from now on you can count on me."

In 1986, the bishop was in Hong Kong as Secretary General of the Conference of Asian Bishops when he suffered a heart attack and had to be hospitalized. Mother Teresa was in the United States at the time, but she sent him a letter in which she asked who had given him permission to get sick! "You should have spoken to your mother about it first," she chided, tongue-in-cheek. "But know that I will pray hard for your recovery." Bishop Henry recounted this anecdote to me several months ago when he was in Flanders for a heart operation.

During his convalescence, we often spoke about you, Bishop Joseph [Raya]. We spoke about your life as bishop in the Holy Land and about your being at Madonna House; about your appointment as Assistant Bishop in Beirut, not long ago, and about your even more recent appointment as Bishop of Marjeijoun in Caesarea Philippi, in Lebanon's Golan Heights. It struck me repeatedly how much there is in Henry D'Souza's life that resembles your own, and I thought it would please you if I shared a bit of it with you.

The archbishop is a deeply religious man who lives in, with, and through Jesus the Lord. You can find him praying at all hours of the night and day in the small chapel next to my guest room here. Adoration before the Blessed Sacrament and the Eucharistic celebration are the heart and soul of his priestly life. Here, in this chapel, with its two typically Flemish glass windows dating from Archbishop Perier's time, he encounters the Eucharistic Jesus.

It is common knowledge that the first question Henry's "foster mother," Mother Teresa, asks whenever visiting the home of a bishop, a convent, or a mission is, "Where is Jesus?" Those who know her well enough realize that she means the chapel with the Eucharistic Presence of the Lord. Being on such intimate terms with the Eucharistic Jesus is, I believe, the source of the special radiation and influence that seems to exude from Henry. I noticed this back in Flanders, and I see it once again here in Calcutta.

The day before his operation last July, we celebrated Mass together in his hospital room. Afterwards, as soon as he had gathered enough strength his first suggestion was that we again celebrate Mass in order to thank Jesus for the many people who had cared for him. Beyond any doubt, the whole nursing staff experienced in him a true man of God.

The handful of Christians in the Archdiocese of Calcutta (a scant 85,000 among a population of 32,000,000!) look upon their bishop with admiration and respect. The man is exceptionally simple and jovial. He fully realizes that evangelization in West Bengal, with its Hindu majority and the presence of so many other non-Christian religions — Jains, Muslims, Buddhists, Sikhs — as well as different Christian denominations is, in the first place, a question of witnessing. Henry D'Souza is listened to because absolutely nothing in his leadership or life is affected or pretentious. Insofar as it is possible, he makes use of the modern techniques of our mass media to proclaim The Message. But it is never done in order to promote his own prestige or to focus attention on himself. The desire to dominate, to exert power or to attract attention never enters his mind. His people realize that he is a deeply religious and humble man, and that is why they see Jesus in him.

Henry is an exceptionally intelligent person. He acquired various academic degrees both at home and abroad.

And many of his family have important positions in various parts of the world. Yet he told me, "When I came back home after completing my theological studies in Rome, my bishop appointed me to a jungle outpost on the fringe of the diocese among a tribe of people whose language I didn't even understand. I lived there in a miserable hut. There was no running water and no electricity. The toilet was off in the jungle. For two years I fought bitterness, indifference and panic. 'What can the bishop be thinking? God knows the Church of India desperately needs intellectuals, and yet he sends me to the illiterate and the primitive!' Such were my initial thoughts. Gradually, however, I came to discover Jesus more and more in my missionary life. I laid my pride aside. Slowly I began to see that my place was there where the Lord sent me. I needed this conversion in order to learn to draw all my strength and joy from Jesus Himself."

During Henry's first visit to our diocese and the city of Bruges where he was going to participate in the Procession of the Precious Blood, I asked him to speak to a group of sick and handicapped religious. When he saw the Sisters, he was very moved. He told them the story of his first mission, and added that the hidden and suffering members of the Church were just as important in God's eyes as an archbishop. The only thing necessary, he said, was to make place for God in one's life and to love Him.

Following the procession, he confided to me how overjoyed he was to have had the chance to carry the relic with the Precious Blood of Jesus through the streets of Bruges. "I prayed the whole time I did it," he said, "thanking Jesus for my poor health and my pastoral work with the poor of Calcutta."

Not long afterwards, he returned to our country, this time for his operation. During the six weeks that he was with us, Joseph, I gave him your books to read: *The Face of God* and *The Eyes of the Gospel* (both published by Dimension Books, Inc., Denville, N.J., the first in 1976 and the other in 1978).

Your thoughts and reflections about God and the Church, about the priesthood and the liturgy deeply impressed him. One evening I discussed with him, at some length, your Byzantine thinking and your own eventful life as a bishop which, as I said, is so much like his. I read for him your own witness as it appears in your "Letter to my Co-Bishops in the United States of America and Canada." You wrote:

> For many years as a priest — and like so many of my fellow priests — I lived in solitude with myself, and in the market-place with others. Like any other priest, I sat at the banquets of sinners and at the tables of the good and the just. I spent years in the silence of administration and on the throne of power and glory. I dined with kings and slept on the bare ground. I ate sumptuously and fasted in front of the Knesset of Israel.

> Like all my fellow priests and bishops, I am fully aware of the need for a simple, childlike message of hope and joy. Our journey to the resurrection is strewn with failure and success, discouragement and enthusiasm, with trials, tribulations, loves and hates. We are creatures of magnificence and destitution, of heartaches and exaltations. We all recognize the need for continual growth.

You are a Semite. Born in Lebanon, brought up by French Sisters, and formed by the White Fathers in Jerusalem. You are steeped in the traditions of your Eastern origins and the Byzantine Church, but our West and our Latin Church are not unfamiliar to you.

D'Souza was born in Calcutta, but his family comes from Goa. The poetry and the gentle playfulness of the Portuguese colonial culture that has marked his lifestyle connect wonderfully with your own sense of the beautiful and your own deep feelings for humanity. His keen power of thought and intellectual formation were completed by the innate sense of art so inherent to his Bengalese surroundings. You would say, "Every artist witnesses to God. Whoever witnesses to God points to beauty."

Henry tries to convey to his people that they must build their faith and their sense of church community on a strongly-lived relationship with God. "We must look at all people and everything through eyes purified by faith," he insists. I told him about how, when you were a pastor in Birmingham, Alabama, you were severely beaten one evening by members of the Ku Klux Klan because of your intimate friendship with Martin Luther King; and how, as Archbishop of Galilee, you went to protest the occupation of two Palestinian villages by the Israeli Army. I also made it a point to tell him how, in all your social and political activities, you remain always a man of God.

You were a bishop in the Holy Land when you wrote about your experiences there:

> During these six years, my whole scientific approach to God melted away. I experienced my kinship with the Lord. I rediscovered my Oriental and Semitic soul. The Fathers of the Desert became alive in my heart. The Fathers of the Church — Basil, Chrysostom, the two Gregorys — these became my daily bread, light and life. Their writings illuminated all that a priest of God wishes to come alive in him. Heaven left my head and came to dwell in my heart. Spiritual riches, like material abundance, are motives for thanks. But those who are really grateful try to share their riches with others.

In 1975 you went to live at Madonna House in Combermere. One day you were rushed to the hospital where you urgently had to undergo a heart operation. In your room there, you wrote a reflection about sickness and death, on life and resurrection. You were also full of praise for the doctors and nursing staff. To them you gave a witness of your love for Jesus. You witnessed to that love in your book: *The Acathist Hymn to the Name of Jesus* (Alleluia Press, 1983).

When Bishop Henry returned from his own heart operation I gave him a copy of this book in which you had rewritten the ancient Acathist Hymn to the Name of Jesus in twelve odes. In the preface you wrote: "Only those who seek a most intimate relationship with the Lord Jesus and those who burn to see His Face can be invited to pray this Office."

Here, in Archbishop Henry's residence, I often talk to him about you and about your great love for Jesus and the people entrusted to your care. Your life is that of a fiery priest who has to answer, in the Church's name, the questions of those in your care, both Christian and non-Christian, and this in sensitive, and often even dangerous, surroundings.

"Where is Jesus?" is not only Mother Teresa's concrete question as she inquires where the Eucharistic Presence is reserved. It is the most important question forming itself in the being of every person. How often I have reflected on this question with Bishop Henry. I have done so with the Sisters of Mother Teresa to whom I am giving some conferences about Catherine Doherty and her spiritual family — that family to which you, too, belong. You, as a bishop, try to live the spirituality of Madonna House in order to witness in a still deeper way that Jesus is the answer to all the questions we pose about life and happiness and truth.

During the last 20 years, I have been able to see how clearly this Jesus is so present in your life, in that of Henry, and of so many other of the bishops I have had the good fortune to meet in the Southern Hemisphere. My own bishop, consecrated two years ago, chose as his motto: "Turn your eyes to Jesus."

In the Acathist Hymn to the Name of Jesus, we pray: "Show me, a sinner, the beauty of Your Face." I have heard you say so often that we, by our identification with Jesus, become His reflection and His transparency. That is why those who look at us can, in a certain sense, see Jesus also.

"It is the meaning of your priesthood to be totally one with Him," Mother Teresa said to me not long ago when we were speaking about our priestly mission. "Let Christ live His life in and through you. Our work consists, then, in showing Him to others. He wants to live His life in you. He wants to look at others through your eyes, go to them with your feet and love them with your heart."

Do you know, dearest brother in Jesus, that I always think of you whenever I hear her speak about His life radiating from us? One day in Madonna House, we asked you very directly, Bishop, "What does belief really mean to you?" With your big, dark eyes, you looked me straight in the face and said, "The risen and glorified Christ who shines at me through you."

In Madonna House one sees many icons. They are in the chapel, in the living and sleeping quarters, and in the workrooms. Often during the Byzantine liturgical celebrations at which you presided, you spoke to us about our own godliness and the Face of Christ in the icons. "They are the mirrors in which we can stare at God," you said. "There are also icons of flesh and blood — our own faces. Whoever cherishes this face in a belief in the risen and glorified Lord touches God. You must regularly dive into the effervescent life of God, as a swimmer into the sea. Then you will be looking at God Himself with the eyes of the Gospels, the

Father, the Son, and the Holy Spirit, and you will be able to look up to every person. You will sing out with joy and happiness." I have tried to pass on to Mother Teresa's Sisters and the novices what you and Catherine Doherty have taught us about the theology of icons and about the beauty of God.

In 1979, a group of publishers approached you with the question: "Who is Jesus Christ for you?" You answered beautifully. I have that answer here. It is something which both Mother Teresa and Archbishop Henry have greatly appreciated. You wrote:

> When I first read the question: "For you, who is Jesus Christ?" my whole being sang a hymn of joy for the opportunity to put into words what was so bright and clear and alive in me. Words are inadequate in telling who a person is and much more so when they attempt to tell who Jesus Christ is. But when there is a song, we have to sing it with our own intonations, deficient though they may be.

> For me, Jesus Christ is, first of all and above all, my God, my Savior and my Lord. He is God, the God of gods, the very God of the very God. He is God, Creator and Possessor of the whole creation. In the language of the Greek Church, I call God the Creator "Poetizing." I say: "I believe in one God 'the Poetizing' of heaven and earth. . . ." To create, for my God, is indeed to compose a poem. He composed a poem and called it "heaven." He composed another poem and called it "earth." And another he called "stars," and another, "water," "animal," and "angels." My God composed an infinite number of poems.

> The most splendid and most thrilling of them all he called "person," "man and woman." In this person, God summarized all of His own power and beauty and all the miracles of the universe, the far away heavens and the

smallest atoms. Man-woman is the mirror that reflects God's glory and grandeur. The human body composed by God is the ultimate expression of His power and beauty. Let us talk foolish, human, talk and say that God cannot create any more miraculous piece of glory than the human person in the flesh, because the human body was obviously destined to be His very own dwelling place, His very Self revealed in that flesh and the channel of the whole of creation's return to its origin, God Himself. The human person is the expression of God's own freedom and glory.

All the poems of my God: every single poem and every part of every poem is also a poem ever fresh, ever new, ever alive that sings and dances and that radiates light and life and the warmth of the resurrection. Every poem reflects the goodness of God. My God has a face that radiates a smile. A name is a mask. A smile reveals a person, Jesus. God can neither be deduced nor induced by philosophical thinking or logic. The Bible itself does not dictate a formula about God. The Bible is a prophetic word which opens yesterday and today in view of a better experience of a God who never ceases to reveal Himself. He did reveal Himself, indeed, and Confucius had a glimpse of Him. Buddha had a glimpse. Old, human cultures such as the Persian, the Chinese, the Egyptian, the African and the American, as well as the Greek and the Roman each had a bright glimpse of the "Incomprehensible" God. Mohammed had a bright glimpse and Moses was all shaken by His reality. Each one of the Prophets of old and each event in the history of Israel in the Bible uncovered a new horizon onto God. And God kept on revealing Himself until one day, when humanity was ready "to see His face and not die," He joined heaven to earth and became man.

God became real man, a man who cried and smiled. A man who suffered and thrilled for joy. A man who hungered and thirsted and whose flesh vibrated with all the love and tenderness and disappointments and triumphs of our humanity. The One who has all names became a human face, and was named Jesus. The invisible became visible. And the untouchable became human flesh, both touchable and touching. God is no more the "One abiding there, somewhere — a pie in the sky," but our Emmanuel, a companion whose human voice carried and revealed the secrets of heaven.

In Jesus the abstract becomes concrete reality and God takes on a smiling countenance, a face that glows with light and goodness. Since Jesus possesses the fullness of divinity, He plays in it His personal experience and in it He moves freely, joyously and with ease. He uses the most daring language to describe God. A Father is a name; a "Daddy" is a face. So Jesus calls God "Abba," "Daddy." Not that "old bachelor who lives in boredom and loneliness" whom Nietzsche accused us of adoring. God is "Abba," eternally generating the Son and breathing the Spirit.

We Christians do not believe in a God. We believe in a God who is Father-Son-Spirit. Thus we do not count numbers: "One," or "Three," or "One in Three," or "Three in One." We point to an ineffable relationship between Persons. We proclaim that there is a relationship of life in God. There is fecundity, generosity, giving and receiving in God. There is love. It is love. . . . He is love.

On this great subcontinent of India, where 78% of the population are Hindus, 11.6% Muslims, 2% Sikhs, and .5% Jains, living with the 3.9% Christians, the first evangelization, the proclamation of Jesus as the Messiah and the Face of God is an urgent task. The essence of our faith in Jesus and the uniqueness of God's self-revelation in Him must be shown to and shared with all peoples. This is the bishop's mission. Archbishop Henry, with his little group of priests, brothers, sisters, catechists and committed lay people, has fully engaged himself in this task.

You have done so, too, Joseph, in your persecuted and ravaged Diocese of Caesarea Philippi in Lebanon, along with your handful of supporters: three priests and 13,000 faithful. You had your 70th birthday recently. Aging has not prevented you from remaining a missionary bishop. For you, Jesus means living and being in Him. You once told me that the Eastern bishops, in the first century, carried the Eucharist around their necks in an icon of Jesus. In this way, they could always show and give Him to the people. The faithful knew that their bishop was a Jesus-bearer.

I told this to Henry and the Sisters. "The bishop is Jesus in our midst," I said. "He is the answer to our search for God. He will help us to turn our eyes to Him and let Him into our hearts." Again, I could connect this to Catherine's Little Mandate:

> Listen to the Spirit — He will lead you.
> Pray always. I WILL BE YOUR REST.

You have helped me, as have Henry and so many other bishops who are truly Christ-bearers, to learn to look to Jesus. Thanks to all of you, I know that the Spirit teaches us how we can descend into the heart of our brothers and sisters. With holy fear we can invite them to look with us upon the splendor of God's Face — to Jesus who, thanks to all of you, has become the source of peace and joy in my own life.

This letter, written from the home of your confrere, Archbishop Henry D'Souza, who has become a real brother to me, as you have, must be read as a sincere expression of my gratitude. In composing this letter, I have highlighted many events from your own biography. You won't begrudge me this, I hope. In my contacts with Mother Teresa and Henry, I have spoken often and expressly about you and told them your life story. I did so because I recognized your life so remarkably in theirs. Or is it because both you and they have radiated the risen and glorified Jesus to me?

I hope that you will be able to stop in Brussels when you leave Lebanon for a few weeks' rest at Madonna House. News from your diocese always interests me. You will also be curious, I suspect, to learn more about Archbishop Henry, Mother Teresa and her Missionaries of Charity in Calcutta. Couldn't we arrange to meet for a few hours then?

Gratefully and affectionately in the risen and glorified Christ,

Omer

LETTER VI:
TABERNACLES OF FLESH

To Geert, General Practitioner

Calcutta, December 14, 1987

Dear Geert,

There were showers last night, and Calcutta is draped in a silvery dew. You can smell the incense and sandalwood in the air — fragrances so typical of India. The first rays of light pierce the misty gauze hanging in the somewhat rose-colored air above the high rows of houses. This fairylike glory of the morning made me recall the talk we had a few weeks ago about the magical quality of India's nature and the whole environment to which you and your wife anticipate coming next year. We talked about Hindu holy books and the Vedic Hymns. They are poetic songs to nature through which the godly comes to us. I suggested that you read the hymn to the goddess of dawn:

> Look, the light arises.
> The most beautiful of all lights. . . .
> Dress. The spirit of life is in you.

Darkness ebbs away and morning takes its place.
He paves the way for the sun and we receive admittance
    to the regions of life.

So it is written in the hymn. Looking at the dew-shrouded light this morning as I made my way to the novitiate of the Missionaries of Charity on Park Street, I thought about this hymn and you. However, the whole day became a confrontation with a world of misery, pain, suffering and death. A world that is a day in, day out reality — one on which I have reflected much today. These thoughts and reflections I would like to share with you in this letter.

At 6 a.m. I celebrated the Eucharist for 120 of the 300 or so novices in Mother Teresa's Congregation, here in Calcutta, and followed it with a conference. After breakfast, we drove to Prem Dan in a dilapidated little car. At times I wasn't sure that it would make it — that it could stand on its four wobbly wheels! It balked regularly in full traffic, to the alarm of the rather elderly chauffeur and the annoyance of the many honking buses, trucks, cars, bicycles and rickshaws crisscrossing left and right. All were madly trying to find a way through the already too busy streets of Calcutta. The Sisters accompanying me never batted an eyelash. Unperturbed they continued to say the rosary aloud, as calmly as if they were back there in their own quiet chapel!

Prem Dan means "Gift of Love" and refers to a large, oblong building complex that was formerly used by the Imperial Chemical Industries until it was given over to Mother Teresa in 1975. As well as providing a roof for the care of children and the mentally handicapped, it also provides accommodations for courses in housekeeping and small crafts, organized for women from the slums. Here in Prem Dan you meet people from various countries of the world who come to offer their services.

Today Sister Agnes was my guide. Her real name is Subashini Das and she comes from Bengal. She was, in 1949, the first to join Mother Teresa as a member of the newly-formed Congregation. She had been one of Mother Teresa's students and wanted to follow her into the slums. She is now Superior of the Motherhouse on Lower Circular Road and is highly respected by all the Sisters.

"We'll stop on the way," she said to me, "to pop into Kalighat, the House of the Dying, and say a prayer in the new chapel just installed on the roof. On a plaque at the entrance you can read: 'Nirmal Hriday,' The Place of the Pure Heart."

Mother Teresa received this house on August 15, 1952 for use in caring for the dying, and she bestowed this name on it the day when her Sisters began their work in it. That was on August 22, the Feast of the Queenship of Mary.

Nirmal Hriday is situated next to the temple of the goddess Kali, the destroyer of life. It formerly served as a shelter for wanderers, pilgrims and ne'er-do-wells. The neighborhood has a disreputable name. Pimps, professional beggars, adventurers, barterers, and hordes of children find a corner here. Several Brothers and Sisters, with some volunteers, were busy cleaning the premises with a strong-smelling, disinfecting lye. In order to do a thorough house-cleaning, they had to evacuate most of the sick from one wing to another. In the midst of all this hustle and bustle, I noticed a very bloated woman, obviously dying, being carried in on a filthy stretcher. One of the Sisters and a young volunteer from Detroit immediately went to help. I had met them yesterday at a gathering for the lay leaders in Chitrabani, a center for the mass media run by the Jesuits of Calcutta.

At the entrance to Nirmal Hriday, in the corner close to the male ward, I saw a framed sign: "Mother's First Love." It couldn't be expressed more simply or clearly. It is here, Geert, in this place, that thousands of deathly sick people have been able to experience God's Love for each of them. For thirty-five years they have experienced this Love in the attention and tender affection of the Missionaries of Charity. But in all that goes on here, thousands of visitors and volunteers have also discovered the healing presence of Jesus for body and soul. Here the Gospel is visible. You only have to feed your believing eyes and heart on it.

Painted in white on the inside of the rear door of the mini-bus that serves as an ambulance for the Sisters (who drive it every morning into the slum areas), I read: "Find Jesus in Kalighat." In this house for the dying you can meet Jesus where He lives — in the emaciated and abandoned dying, whom Mother Teresa calls "tabernacles of flesh."

"How our lives would change," she says, "if we could only take Jesus at His word: 'I was hungry. I was alone, sick and imprisoned, and you did all this for Me.' Have we visited Him in His tabernacles of flesh? Do we also see them in our comfortable homes — or do they only exist for a silent, suffering Lord Who, on earth, has no other hands than ours — no other words than ours? How many handicapped, mentally ill and desperate young people are not cared for in our hospitals? How many aren't there right there in our neighborhoods? Do we ever pay them a visit? Do we go to share Jesus' crucifixion in them? Jesus said: 'If you want to be My followers, you must take up My cross and follow Me.' By that He meant that we should help carry His cross and feed Him in those who suffer hunger, clothe Him in those who are naked, shelter Him in our own homes. Once we have poured out our hearts in love and given our hands in service, then only will we become true contemplatives. We will see God in the heart of the world. We will touch Christ twenty-four hours a day."

This morning we meditated, with a group of novices, on some words of Catherine Doherty, about whom I have so often spoken to you. They are in her Little Mandate:

Take up My cross (their cross) and follow Me — going to the poor — being poor — being one with them — one with Me.

Catherine once wrote a beautiful, mythological story called *How Ugly Lady Pain Became So Beautiful.* I told it to the young sisters. She said that from the beginning of time Lady Pain was queen of a vast kingdom. Whenever people really looked into her eyes, they seemed to be a hopeless and dull black. Her face was lined and filled with all of the ugliness in the world. She wore strange, dark garments which merged with the darkness which seemed to follow her everywhere.

Few people wished to behold her for long. If she moved in on them or stopped to look at them they did everything they could to remove her from their presence because wherever she went she brought severe pain — often pain that drove men mad or sent them to an early grave. However, few escaped her. At one time or another, in every person's life, she would come to visit them. She would take the person, hold him tightly, and only let him go when he was quite dead. She was truly Lady Pain, queen of a vast domain.

It happened that one moonlight night she found herself in a garden of olive trees. From afar, she saw a Man kneeling before a stone in utter exhaustion. She moved closer and beheld on the Man's face a pain that was not of her own making. This fascinated her so that she moved closer, close enough to see that beads of blood were trickling down the Man's very pale face. She couldn't understand all this.

Just as the Man saw her, an angel all in white came to Him and held a shining chalice to His lips. The Man drank from it and, over the rim, He smiled at Lady Pain. This amazed her as no one had *ever* smiled at her before!

Then there was a lot of noise and commotion, and a large crowd came into the garden. A man came and kissed the Man she had been watching and He was taken away. Lady Pain just had to follow and see what was going on. Some force greater than herself compelled her to do so. Gradually she lost sight of Him and she was greatly distraught. Her heart beat wildly over her loss. She had to find that Man. She had to find the Man who had smiled at her through His pain.

She found Him being flogged and tortured by Roman soldiers. It was impossible to understand what was happening to her because, now, she wanted to stop this suffering — to put her own thin body between Him and the whips. But she could not do so. Just then the Man lifted His head and, as their eyes met, He smiled at her again. She covered her face and wept. Later, when they mocked and crowned Him with thorns, she was angry. She *cared*! She wanted to stop these men from doing all of these things, but was powerless to do so. When they took Him inside a building she left disconsolately.

Time passed, and she found herself on a hill on which there were three crosses. On one of them she saw the Man being crucified. She was unable to endure the pain of seeing that dying Man. She ran to the foot of His cross and started to tear the heavy nails from His feet. His blood fell upon her head. It ran down her face and onto her garments. She saw that they had been dyed ruby red.

Slowly she walked away and sat down by the side of a lake to rest. She looked and saw her face reflected upon its waters. But she did not recognize herself! What had happened? She — ugly Lady Pain — was beautiful! In some way her eyes had been purified and she saw beyond her ugliness to the beauty within.

"And that," Catherine used to say, "is why, ever since, men who are able to see more deeply know that Love wedded itself to Lady Pain, and that Love can make her beautiful — as beautiful as she saw herself on the day of Love's crucifixion."

In symbolic language, Catherine Doherty says that every pain receives another form through the encounter with Love on the cross. Whoever looks at misery and the suffering of people with the eyes of faith knows that Jesus is present in all pain and suffering in order to renew His own suffering in us. For all those who believe in this suffering Jesus, everything that lives and breathes takes on a personal dimension. Everything is ultimately united to Him, Jesus the Lord. That's why our cross is also the cross of the poor, that is to say, of every person, because it is all together that we carry the Calcutta of sickness and suffering, of sin, loneliness, selfishness, and thirst for God in us. Therefore, a remarkable union and solidarity exists in physical and spiritual suffering.

With your long medical experience, Geert, you know as well as I do, that the only way we, on our pilgrimage through life, can walk with any fruit is the Way of the Cross — our own cross and the cross of our brothers and sisters, the cross of Christ Himself. Isn't it because of this cross and in order to alleviate the sufferings of others, that you decided, as a young man, to become a doctor? But this suffering is Jesus' very own pain in each of us. It is striking that Catherine Doherty and Mother Teresa both wanted to encounter and love Jesus by sharing His pain and suffering in the evil, the misery, and the hunger of His people.

What goes on here, in Nirmal Hriday, in and through the unlimited and heroic love of the Missionaries of Charity for these human derelicts, these "tabernacles of flesh," must be explained from a similar experiencing of the mystery of suffering and death. Isn't it also from within this same mystery that you, as a believing doctor, view the concrete reality of your own life? I know only too well that you not only make accurate diagnoses in your daily practice, but that you are also helped and supported by your deeply religious wife, Kate, and that you try to carry the cross of our persecuted, humiliated and crucified God in the sick who come to you. About such things you seldom speak, but your friends and patients realize that you experience it as such.

Today I talked quite a bit to the Sisters about this mystery of the cross that played such an important role in the life of Catherine Doherty. What she said about the suffering Christ will undoubtedly speak to you, Geert. That's why I would like to cite a letter that she wrote to her spiritual family in May of 1978:

> Christ is in agony until the end of the world. But Christ is in you and me. And what is more important, in the other fellow, too. What about them being in agony, my brothers and sisters?
>
> That, my friend, is what Madonna House is all about. Open your hearts. You have the key to do it. The Lord has given it to you in baptism. Open your heart and let Him in. Stop thinking about yourself and begin — honestly, truthfully, totally — thinking of others.
>
> What does it matter that you and I may become martyrs! That is the crown of faith and Christianity. I doubt if any one of us, including myself, will have earned it. There is no question of bloody martyrs. There is only the question

of white martyrdom. The martyrdom of listening. The martyrdom of consoling. The martyrdom of loving. The martyrdom of hoping, for oneself and for others. The martyrdom of total surrender to God through the other, whoever he or she might be. Prepare yourselves to serve God in totality.

In Staff Letter 104, in 1962, she had also written about the cross:

> I cannot visualize a love story with God without a cross. To me the cross is *THE Thing*. I desire it; I accept it. I ask for the grace never to fear it because, at the end, I shall finally know its joy.

> Of course the cross is there. When I talked about the cross I think you may have misunderstood what I meant. For me the cross is the key to Him whom my heart loves. Without the cross there is no Easter! Unless I die on the cross, I cannot see Him in heaven. I must lie on the cross that He made for me. It is certainly not the one I am making for myself.

> God embraced the cross for us because He wanted to. For this He was born. For this we are born also: to lie on it with Him. I mean these words literally, but I think you don't understand me, and that is the problem. Think of your vocation as the glory of the cross, what He has done for us.

More than once I heard Catherine Doherty, in her noon spiritual reading at Madonna House in Combermere, say that we must hang on to the other side of the cross if we want to understand the suffering of Jesus in mankind and help Him to bear it.

Here in Calcutta one is continually confronted with this cross and this suffering. The severely handicapped, the disfigured, and those unsightly sick people are, in our western countries, safely cared for in well-equipped institutions. Here you see many of them on the sidewalks, or propped up against buildings and miserable huts. Every morning people go through the still-silent streets in order to collect those who are lying there dying and bring them to Nirmal Hriday.

In our lands, it is possible to ignore or avoid those who are visibly suffering. In Calcutta they literally lie before your very door. It forces you to reflect. The words uttered on the cross: "I thirst!" take on a deeper significance. It is impossible to separate them from the spirituality of either Catherine Doherty or of Mother Teresa. You can read them next to every cross hanging above the altar in any of the houses of the Missionaries of Charity. Usually the words, "I quench" are to be found under the cross. The exceptional thing, though, here in the House of the Dying, is that your heart brims over with a joy that is difficult to put into words when you see the cross with all its human suffering.

Yesterday Mother Teresa told me: "You now find Jesus in the Blessed Sacrament also present on the roof of Kalighat. Next to the small chapel we are building a few rooms for our Sisters who will live close to the dying and close to Jesus." I went there to pray with Sister Agnes. I prayed for you and Kate and the children, for all the sick in whom you try to alleviate Jesus' suffering and pain, with your whole soul, heart, and body. On the roof itself lay quite a few people, either sick or utterly exhausted, waiting to find a place in which to rest or to die in peace. Sisters care for them. Tucked into the leather belt that they wear under their blue and white sari is a cross. Every morning, as they dress, the Sisters kiss this cross with the words: "Let this cross remind me that I am the bride of the crucified Jesus. That is why I, as a Missionary of Charity, in all that I do, lead the life of the crucified, and carry out His work only."

In one of the large rooms on the ground floor, I saw a young Sister sitting by an old, emaciated woman. She pressed her so lovingly against her, and caressed her hand. I stood by speechless, silent and respectful before the wonder that was taking place before my eyes in this House of Death — and Life. "Jesus performs miracles every day," Mother Teresa had said to me last year during her visit to Flanders. Then she recounted the story of a young man in a New York prison who was suffering from AIDs:

> I was in New York visiting my Sisters and the Priest-Missionaries of Charity not long ago. I received a telephone call from the head of one of the prisons urgently requesting me to come to see one of the prisoners who was suffering from AIDS. I went there with a few of the Sisters, but they were rudely shown the door by this young man. "It is you I need," he shouted. "And no one else!" I went to sit beside him and he began his story:

> "I'm in my early 20s, Sister. It seems that I've been baptized, but neither God nor His Church could ever move me. Now I sit here with many crimes to my record. But I want to confide something to you. I have AIDS and I don't have much longer to live. Whenever I have heavy pain in the palms of my hands, I think of the nails with which they crucified Jesus. Whenever the pain moves up into my head and back, I see in my imagination the hostage, Jesus, with His crown of thorns. And I speak to Him. Sister, I'm going to die, and I would like to do it with you. Take me to your house."

At Mother Teresa's insistence, the prison director agreed to entrust the young man to her so that he could prepare for his death in peace, reconciled to God. She brought the youth back with her to the Sisters' house in New York.

When he entered the house where our sisters give refuge to AIDS patients, he fell to his knees and began to pray to Jesus. You must hate sin, Father, but love sinners. Jesus works miracles every day, as He did with this young man. But in order to see them, you must have a simple and pure heart.

Nirmal Hriday, the *Place of the Pure Heart*. Next year (or so I hope), you will visit this place with Kate. For you also, this direct contact with the love, so visibly present here in the mystery of the cross, will be — as it is for me today — a moment of special grace. The moment of emptying of everything that, through our self-conceit, pride and selfishness, blinds us and prevents us from looking at people with the eyes of a pure heart.

Last year I received a letter from another doctor friend who regularly spends his weeks of vacation working here with Mother Teresa's houses. He sent it from Kalighat with a volunteer who was returning home, and it was a profound witness of what he experienced. He wrote:

The misery here is sometimes unbearable, and yet we experience such an intense joy. This afternoon we experienced something truly very exceptional. We are here with different nationalities: Finns, Americans, French, Dutch, English, Belgians. One young man in the group had been intensely busy the whole day with a dying person. Neither of the two could understand a word of the other's language. But in the afternoon the young man had an idea. He brought his guitar and began to strum it softly for his patient. Everyone became absolutely still. And most of them approached more closely in order to hear the music.

Slowly they all began to hum along, until everyone was singing. It grew in crescendo. All the sick, with the exception of two who were dying, were sitting up. The Sisters present, along with the rest of us, were so under the influence of what was going on that we left everything to join in. We sang for a whole hour. I can't begin to describe it. We hummed "Nearer My God to Thee . . . Nearer to Thee . . .!" and slowly drifted back to our work, carrying on with it in utter silence. This was a moment pregnant with love. This is love! Two or more hearts united in song! Something like this can only happen in Kalighat.

Dr. Jan lives and works — as you do, Geert — in the spirit of Mother Teresa. For him, as for you, Lady Pain is a daily companion in the many tabernacles of flesh that are entrusted to his care and professional knowledge by the suffering Jesus. Both of you are extensions of what Mother Teresa's Sisters and the many volunteers do in Calcutta.

Much later in the day we arrived in Prem Dan with Sister Agnes. What I saw there I will save to share with a young nurse who hopes to come here to help next year.

At the end of this day of reflection, Mother Teresa gave me a pamphlet about the Missionaries of Charity. "I sent copies to the kings of Belgium and of Spain," she said spontaneously. I'll bring a copy of it for you and Kate when we meet again in a few weeks' time. In spirit and in heart both of you already belong to these Lay Missionaries.

The day was filled with emotion. From Mother Teresa's house I also went to the banks of the Hooghly River, which separates Calcutta from Howrah. It was sunset. The horizon was tinted a purple-red and a tender glow lay over the water. Again my thoughts turned to our talk about the Vedic Hymns, this time to the verses about the night:

Chase the wolf and the she-wolf. Drive away the thief and the wretch, O queen of the waves. Protect our crossing.

See! The darkness, enwrapped in her folding, black garment, nears. Let her enter, O glory of the morning, as a shield of trust.

> *Affectionate greetings to Kate and the children.*
> *From a pleasantly warm day in Calcutta,*

Omer

WE ARE NOT SOCIAL WORKERS

To Sister Aline, Carmelite

Calcutta, December 16, 1987

Dear Sister Aline,

You mustn't be surprised to receive this letter from me here in Calcutta.

This morning I had a talk with Mother Teresa, who said to me for the umpteenth time, "Father, we are not social workers. We didn't become Missionaries of Charity merely in order to go to the poorest of the poor and stand by their sides in their bodily and material misery. We are religious. We are contemplatives in the world. Speak about this to my Sisters today when you lead them in meditation and prayer."

In preparation for the days of recollection I am giving here (in which you are, in a certain sense, indirectly involved), I once again read the texts about contemplation and the Carmelite life that you gave me last year during my visit to your cloister in Montreal. Following my every stay in the guest house for priests at Madonna House in Combermere, I try never to miss an opportunity to highlight my visit by stopping to celebrate the Eucharist with your little community of 20 Carmelites in Montreal. Your cloister lies discreetly tucked in among ordinary homes, on the corner of a square in the Avenue du Carmel.

Twenty-seven years ago, I came to spend some time with you in order to learn to lead a life of prayer and detachment. After Mass we often discussed the Church in general and our priestly and cloistered lives in particular. "We must live in the heart of the world Church," you said to me during my visit, "united with all of you in the life of God Himself. This is our vocation."

In 1982, on the occasion of the 400th anniversary of the Carmelite reformer and doctor of the Church, Teresa of Avila, a Canadian television network released an interview with you about contemplation and cloistered life. It was discussed for a long time afterwards. In it you revealed how, on one fine day, Jesus entered your life. You said:

> I wanted to proclaim the love of the Crucified Jesus. I wanted to belong completely to Him and He to me. This was my hope and burning desire. That's why I left everything. I wanted to witness to Him through my silence and my seclusion, through my open and receptive hands during prayer. I have no voice. I haven't the slightest power or influence because I possess nothing; I am absolutely poor, but this is the essence of my life. Jesus grows in me as I become smaller. According to worldly standards, I am utterly unimportant and useless in this materialistic society of ours. But I know that I am growing in His image and that I am answering His desires and His calling.

Your life, dear Sister Aline, is a life of contemplation, prayer and penance. However, as I read in the folder you once sent me about life in Carmel:

Contemplation doesn't consist in smiling at the clouds, as so many people seem to think. It is accepting with a simple heart that God is sometimes so frighteningly near and often so very overwhelming.

Doesn't simplicity of heart consist in this being able to accept our human condition in its fundamentally spiritual dimension? Who would dare to insist that dedicating your life to this spiritual dimension is useless? Who doesn't desire to be inspired by the heroic simplicity to which these Carmelites witness with their lives, amidst the passions, the stresses of work, and the daily activities that so often weigh one down?

What Mother Teresa teaches her Sisters is so similar to what is written about your own life in Carmel and to what Catherine Doherty says about the essential element of our union with God. It is about these things that I would like to talk to you in this letter.

Life is obedience to Jesus Christ. It is exercising the evangelical counsels, while we pray vigilantly, meditate day and night on the law of the Lord. This is the heart of the Carmelite rule of life. Carmelites desire to bind themselves to God in faith and humility, walking in the footsteps of the Virgin Mary, who is Mother and Queen of Carmel. To be present in the Church as a heart that listens to His Word in utter quiet; as a fruitful soil that gives place to the Spirit; as a song of praise and supplication that Jesus' life may carry fruit and bring our world to the Father. This is the Carmelite vocation in a nutshell.

I read the text you gave me and I couldn't help comparing it to Catherine Doherty's words in her Little Mandate: "Pray . . . fast . . . pray always . . . fast." How very similar these messages are! The importance of prayer and contemplation for the lay apostolate is strongly emphasized in Madonna House.

The role that Catherine Doherty played in the vocation of Thomas Merton is often mentioned. You know that Merton worked with her awhile in New York. It was Catherine who told him that he would do better to lead a purely contemplative life. Merton became a Trappist monk and penned many important books about the contemplative vocation. One of the things he wrote was:

> Contemplation is essentially an experience of our divine sonship. It is an experiential recognition, a "taste," an interior awakening, an intimate and personal appreciation of the truth that God loves us not only as our Creator but as our Father. More, that He is actually present to us as our "Father," that is, as the source of our supernatural life, our charity. (*Thomas Merton on Prayer*, John J. Higgins, S.J., Doubleday, NY, 1973)

I have often heard Catherine Doherty speak about the Triune God who dwells within us. In our "Way of Life," the Constitutions of Madonna House, Catherine writes:

> I would like to bring to the family that God has deigned to establish through me the very essence of my spirituality . . . the Trinity . . . which takes its root, of course, from Eastern Spirituality. To me (the Trinity) is a reality of faith. The Trinity is fire, flame, movement. The Trinity dwells within me. I am Its temple. The tips of the wings of the Spirit, in this movement, in this fire, touch the tip of my heart. I appear to be standing in the eye of this fantastic creative movement and fire.

In her book, *The Gospel Without Compromise* (Ave Maria Press, Notre Dame, IN, 1976), she says:

> The Eternal Community is the Trinity. It has existed eternally, having no beginning and no end. The Community of the Trinity is simply the Community of Love: God the Father loving God the Son, and this love bringing forth the Holy Spirit.
>
> In order to form a community, man must make contact with the Trinity first. Then, and only then, can he make a community with his fellowmen.

The Carmelite spiritual writers and mystics, Thomas Merton, Catherine Doherty and Mother Teresa all speak in a very similar way about the contemplation of God in our lives. In the Constitutions of the Missionaries of Charity I read:

116. Contemplation of God is a gift of God to every Missionary of Charity,

  — created in the image and likeness of God with a natural power to know and live God as a human being,
  — drawn deeper into the Mystery of His very life and love through Baptism as a child of God,
  — called to the intimacy of His love as the Spouse of Jesus Crucified.

117. Our Life of contemplation is simply to realize,

  — God's constant presence and His tender love for us in the least little things of life. . . .

It must have struck you already, Sister Aline, that all of the words the spiritual writers use to describe their own contemplative tendencies and to motivate others have so much in common with all literature that has love as its theme. "It is a question of Love," Teresa of Avila said when speaking about contemplative life. Little Therese of Lisieux once said, during a crisis of faith: "It is as if I can no longer believe in eternal life. Everything is sliding away from under my feet; only love remains. I don't believe there will be any judgment for those who love. God will hasten to reward His own Love that He sees in their hearts. In the measure that one surrenders to Love, one becomes consumed by this Love."

Catherine Doherty often observed that contemplation is the contemplation of a Person. We contemplate God. Often she likened the contemplation to two lovers sitting on a park bench holding one another's hands and looking deeply into one another's eyes, loving each other wordlessly. Again she has compared it to a woman and a man just silently contemplating each other after the marriage act when both lie still and gaze upon each other in silence. Many times she told us that we will only be able to pray if we are in love with God. She often repeated that the marriage bed of Christ is His cross and said: "Who, in his right mind, wants to fall in love with someone hanging on a cross? Who wants to hang on the other side of that cross? But if we do, if we realize that the cross is our marriage bed, we will experience an indescribable joy."

During our times of reflection today, I spoke to the Sisters of Mother Teresa about contemplation as the essence of their vocation. I directed their attention to all of these people I have just mentioned as being persons who were very much in love with God. And, quoting Thomas Merton's words, I invited them to "live in this love and joy, in the love of Christ and in contemplation, because in this way we will discover ourselves and others as we truly are."

In one of the chapters of her Constitutions, Mother Teresa treated contemplation and prayer as follows:

118. We are called to be contemplatives in the heart of the world by

    a) seeking the face of God in everything, everyone, everywhere, all the time, and His hand in every happening, and especially

    b) seeing and adoring the Presence of Jesus

        — in the lowly appearance of Bread, and
        — in the distressing disguise of the poor, by praying the work, that is doing it with Jesus, for Jesus and to Jesus.

During these days of reflection I joined the Sisters every day in their adoration. Mother Teresa confided to me that the number of requests to join the Congregation has increased by leaps and bounds since the decision was made (back in the '70s) to set aside a time for daily adoration in all of their communities. She said that their daily adoration time gave them the opportunity to sit at the feet of Our Lord; that it was used by them to deepen their belief in Jesus, their love for Him, their gratitude to Him and their rehabilitation in Him to whom they belong. She said that the Sisters spend at least two hours a day in adoration before the Blessed Sacrament.

Every Friday the Eucharist is exposed for the entire day. These hours of prayer, she said, are a special time to do penance for sins and to make supplication for the needs of the world. "We are there," she said, "to bring the sins of the sick and suffering mankind entrusted to us before the converting and healing power of the Eucharistic Christ."

If you enter any of Mother Teresa's houses, you will see busy Sisters at work with buckets and mops. They are active in the kitchen or the dispensary, or they are praying in the chapel. It is my deep conviction that the joy that radiates from their faces finds its source in this contemplative meeting with Jesus in the Eucharist.

"How can you persist, day after day, in caring for all of these destitute and dying people with so much love — these people whom you continually say are Jesus in disguise? On what do you base this belief and conviction?" I once asked Mother Teresa.

"The secret of our lives is very simple, Father," she answered. "Every morning we feed ourselves with the Body and Blood of God in the Eucharistic celebration. He strengthens and fills us with His Life and Love. The work we do, and the spirit in which we go to the poorest of the poor, is an immediate result of this encounter."

Prayer is, for her, the inner continuation of the Eucharist. It exteriorizes itself in the concrete service of the poor.

Catherine Doherty, when questioned about the deeper motivation of her life in the service of the lay apostolate, in the experience of a lived poverty and contemplation, often said:

> All things can be endured and all things become possible between two Masses: the Mass of yesterday and the Mass of tomorrow. . . . I need to be able to sustain one day of my life. I need that food if I am to live His commandments. . . . I need Him daily because I am a sinner and weak.

We must not receive the sacrament of penance for our personal conversion alone, but also in order to beg, for all mankind, the grace of the mercy of reconciliation, reconciliation with God and with others. I write this to you, Sister Aline, because I have heard hundreds of confessions during these days of recollection. I have not had such an experience in Europe for years. This hearing of confessions consumes much time because the Sisters also want to take advantage of the opportunity to seek spiritual direction and to meet, in all simplicity, Jesus Himself in the priest. This seemed an ideal occasion for the Sisters to spend time before the Blessed Sacrament exposed, while waiting their turn for confession. All of this would certainly seem strange to those who don't strive to love Jesus in a most intimate way in their lives.

But Christianity is no purely social or philosophical system. It is actually a personal relationship with the Triune God who, in Jesus, His Son, has become mankind's dearest friend. Called and chosen by this Jesus, we have accepted to live exclusively through and for Him, living and dying in the service of His people.

Whenever I consider your life in Carmel and that of the Sisters here in Calcutta, I am — time and time again — struck by the radicalism of your commitment. You have no occasion to escape the consequences of a love-life with God. The day's rationing of prayer, meditation and work permits no halfway giving of self, no mere formalism. Without contemplation and the Eucharist, prayer and penance, one could easily slide back into a compromise with the world that we have left behind. For all of you who live this life of prayer, poverty and total self-renunciation, it is a source of deep joy. For those of us who merely catch a glimpse of it from time to time, it is a hint at what could be and a challenge to also experience our own vocation as priests and lay people in a true and honest way.

I have often spoken to the Sisters in Mother Teresa's Motherhouse about the Prayer of the Heart and, in this connection, explained the Jesus Prayer to them. Catherine wrote and talked about this prayer a lot. She always said that it was important to "fold the wings of the intellect," as she put it, from time to time. She said that as long as prayer remains a thing of the understanding, it falls short. It is necessary to descend from the head to the heart and to place your understanding in your heart. Prayer then, she said, becomes a prayer of the heart. Not just from one sense, but from the whole being — soul, spirit and body.

Catherine often spoke of her own Russian prayer tradition. In her book, *Soul of My Soul* (Ave Maria Press, Notre Dame, IN, 1985), she wrote:

> Russian Christians don't know anything about yoga, mantras, special breathing, and all the prayers of the non-Christian East. Nor did the Greek monks. They prayed the Jesus Prayer naturally, and the Russians learned it from them: "Lord Jesus Christ, Son of the living God, have mercy on me a sinner," in and out, in and out. You don't do it consciously. It just happens. This is the Jesus prayer.

I must honestly confess that it isn't easy to speak about prayer to religious whose whole lives have become a prayer. They are the ones who practice prayer because they pray continually. There are the hours of silent worship and the hours of community prayer. The many prayers that they know by heart and pray before and after every spiritual exercise as well as the rosary. Do you know that the Sisters here in Calcutta always say the rosary when they are going anywhere?

I gave the Sisters another of Catherine Doherty's texts for reflection today:

People ask me how I pray. It is always hard to answer such questions, but I do my best because I know that "prayer is a hunger," in the words of Father Edward Farrell. And my brothers and sisters are as hungry for it as I am.

I fell in love with God when I was six. This may seem like an exaggeration, but it isn't. God was close to me in the same way that one child is close to another. . . .

I proceeded slowly, even painstakingly, to vocal prayers. Suddenly these were left behind and I found myself in a new land — the land of meditation. I always compare it to going to a dance and finding a boyfriend who deeply attracts you. You remember and savor every word that he says. My lover was Christ, and I read the Gospel avidly, meditating on each word. The Gospel became my favorite prayer.

But the land of meditation was also a temporary one. Meditation fell away as old clothes, and now I was clad in the beautiful garments of contemplation. Life was entirely different now. It seemed as if the Lord Himself were explaining things to me. . . . I was lost in God in those days.

Where does one go after being "lost in God"? The answer is a strange one, difficult to understand. You will not be able to understand it with your head, only with your heart. What happened now was that I myself became a prayer.

A person who is a prayer is someone deeply in love with the Word. He is deeply in love with a Person. . . . Far from interfering with your life, "being a prayer" makes you very meticulous about doing little things well for the love of God. (From *Soul of My Soul*, Ave Maria Press, Notre Dame, IN, 1985)

I have been able to spend many hours praying here with Mother Teresa and her Sisters. I have thanked Jesus because you and your Carmelite Sisters and these Missionaries of Charity are so strongly and visibly united in Jesus by your life of prayer.

I also spoke to the Sisters about the experience of *poustinia*, as this way of prayer is practiced at Madonna House. Many of the members of Madonna House spend 24 hours a week at one of the many small hermitages there. They go there with the Bible only and fast and pray. In a commentary on the crisis within the Church during the '60s, Catherine Doherty wrote:

> I have only one answer to all of these problems — my *poustinia.* This means prayer, penance, dying to oneself, loneliness and silence. I want to carry all these things before God in a spirit of love and rehabilitation, as the prophets did. In the *poustinia*, I can intercede, before God, for all our fellowmen, our brothers and sisters in Christ whom we, in Madonna House, love so passionately.

I also spoke about the *poustinia* of the heart to the many Sisters present here today. I quoted from the little book entitled *Madonna House at Prayer* by Father Richard Starks, a priest of Madonna House Apostolate (Dimension Books, Denville, NJ, 1977). He wrote:

> Catherine's Mandate says distinctly, "Go into the marketplace and stay with Me." This means that we will move from the *poustinia* experience into the fiber of society with our apostolate. We must take her seriously when Catherine says that this *poustinia* is not primarily a geographical place, but that it is first of all within men's hearts. And if they carry that spirit of Gospel-Word and prayer and fasting into their work, then they are being faithful to that other line of the Mandate which beckons

them to "preach the Gospel WITH YOUR LIFE — WITHOUT COMPROMISE." If your family members embrace this idea of the *poustinia* in the market place, then, as Catherine says:

"slowly, imperceptibly, the world around them will change. For the silence within them will become part of God's loving, mighty, creative, fecund silence, and His voice will be theirs . . . and the light of it will become a light to their neighbor's feet. Thus silence will bring peace — to all. And the prayer of silence will be heard in our land, far and wide."

To conclude this day of recollection, we knelt for a full hour in adoration before the Blessed Sacrament. I was blessed to spend it next to Mother Teresa. From time to time, I interrupted the silence to read aloud a few of Catherine Doherty's prayers. Before singing the song of praise to the Blessed Sacrament, I recited an excerpt from Thomas Merton. For years he had imagined God saying to him:

And when you have been praised a little and loved a little, I will take away all of your gifts and your love and your praise and you will be utterly forgotten and abandoned, and you will be nothing, a dead thing, a rejection. And in that day you shall begin to possess the solitude you have so long desired. And your solitude will bear immense fruit in the souls of men whom you will never see on earth.

Do not ask when it will be or where it will be or how it will be: . . . It does not matter. So do not ask me, because I am not going to tell you. You will not know until you are in it.

But you shall taste the true solitude of my anguish and my poverty and I shall lead you into the high places of my joy and you shall die in Me. (*Thomas Merton on Prayer* by John Higgins, S.J., Doubleday, NY, 1973)

This is the language of contemplation — a language that is understood by those who pray and fast. This language is understood by all of you over there in the Carmel in Montreal, where you pray day and night to Jesus, your Beloved. You pray for us in the Low Lands by the North Sea, for Catherine Doherty's spiritual family in Combermere, and for the Missionary Sisters of Charity in Calcutta. Thomas Merton in his *Seeds of Contemplation* (Dell Publishing Co., NY, 1968) says:

> The highest vocation in the Kingdom of God is that of sharing one's contemplation with others and bringing other men to the experiential knowledge of God that is given to those who love Him perfectly. But the possibility of mistake and error is just as great as the vocation itself.
>
> In the first place, the mere fact that you have discovered something of contemplation does not yet mean that you are supposed to pass it on to somebody else. *Contemplatio aliis tradere* implies two vocations: one to be a contemplative, and another still to teach contemplation. Both of them have to be verified.
>
> But then, as soon as you think of yourself as teaching contemplation to others you make another mistake. No one can teach contemplation except God Who gives it. The best you can do is write or say something that will serve as an occasion for someone else to realize what God wants of him.

This morning, as I entered the house on Lower Circular Road, I noticed a small sign next to the steps with the words of Mother Teresa written on it: "Thank God from the depths of your heart that He has chosen you to live for Him forever."

It is out of gratitude for your and my vocations, the love-adventure of our lives in and with God, the ever-unique reality of our existence, that I wanted to write to you so freely in this letter. Share my gratitude with your Sisters, whom I respectfully and affectionately greet from Calcutta.

Omer

LETTER VIII:

GOD CANNOT FILL WHAT IS ALREADY FULL

To Brenda, Nurse

Calcutta, December 19, 1987

Dear Bren,

I promised myself to make free time to write to you from Calcutta where, for a few weeks, I am the happy guest of Mother Teresa and Archbishop Henry D'Souza.

On the plane that brought me from Amsterdam to Calcutta (a flight of 12 long hours!) I had ample time to do quite a lot of reading. Among the reading material that I had was a copy of the French newspaper *Le Monde*. It carried a report and commentary on a gathering of several thousand young people in Paris. In this gathering, they discussed their relationship with the Church. I also had with me a book, written in letter form, by the French journalist, Georges Suffert (*Lettre ouverte aux gens de vingt ans a qui l'on ment*, Albin Michel, Paris, 1977). This can be roughly translated as: *An Open Letter to Twenty-Year-Olds to Whom We Are Lying*. In this book, the author tries to answer honestly the question of a young man: "Why are people in their fifties so incommunicative? Why are they so laconic when it comes to subjects like happiness, politics, love? Of what good is their life experience if they are so ashamed of it?"

Suffert remarks:

> The young man didn't want an historic explanation from me. He was simply curious to know how we can manage to get up in the morning, go to work, eat, return home, conceive children, exercise our voting privilege, pray to God, or explain why we don't believe in Him. Not such stupid concerns. In this open letter to you young people, who are all too often manipulated, I have tried to explain why we middle-aged folk have not always proved so exemplary. But I also wanted to show that you young people can sometimes be rather audacious and naive in the way in which you make your well-meant observations and manifestos. I wanted, above all, to convince you that the happiness you seek isn't actually all that far away. . . .

> I read in *Le Monde*:

> Christian educators can't quite believe their eyes. The search for a clear, Christian profile on the part of our youth today is genuinely sincere and more present among our young people than we would ever think. Such a phenomenon was unimaginable four or five years ago. They are full of admiration for the singer, Madonna, and Mother Teresa, Edith Piaf and the Cure of Ars. On a religious level they, in no way, want to be strait-jacketed. If they resent a religious upbringing or a compulsory attendance at Mass, they say so straightforwardly. But when they do believe in God, they also say so openly....

It is not my intention, Bren, to send you a psychological or sociological treatise about the faith of modern day youth.

I only too readily admit that I am not at all familiar with their lifestyle and way of thinking. But because of my deep affection for you and those of your generation, I would like to share some of the things that I have experienced here, and how I have meditated upon them.

In this exciting city where life and death, good and evil, poverty and riches are to be found side by side, I have seen and listened to many young men and women of your age. They have also posed questions, and I have tried to answer them. They expect this from their elders, or from those who have had several decades more of life experience than they, and we must not answer their questions with silence.

Many young people come to Calcutta from all corners of the world. They include tourists, adventurers, and people searching for the meaning of their existence, for the meaning of suffering and death, of love and happiness. You meet many of them in the guest house of the YWCA, the Young Women's Christian Association, here. This is a modest little hostel on Middleton Row set up for young people who have to travel on a limited budget. The YWCA also does a lot of charitable and social work here in Calcutta. Young people are welcomed there in a truly Christian and hospitable way. This is really very important, especially for those who come to work in Mother Teresa's houses.

Many of these young people came to Calcutta as sightseers, or were simply passing through en route to one or another country in the Far East. Then, deeply impressed by what they saw going on at Mother Teresa's houses, they decided to spend some time here. Some of them I encountered in Shishu Bhavan, the Children's Home, in Nirmal Hriday, the Home for the Dying, and in Prem Dan, the former factory of the Indian Chemical Industries where physically and mentally handicapped persons are cared for. You see them, with the forthrightness and spontaneity so typical of youth, bathing the sick and caring for them in other ways. They cut their hair, shave them and help to feed them. With sweat dripping from their faces in the oppressive heat of this humid tropical climate, they collect food and help to distribute provisions and clothing.·

You meet them in the deep silence of Kalighat where they simply keep vigil with the dying. You see them again in the Motherhouse chapel on Lower Circular road where they participate in the one to two hours of adoration daily. For many of them, this stay is a difficult and sobering confrontation with one aspect of reality — the world of misery and poverty with which they are so unfamiliar. All the pictures and stories they have seen, heard or read in magazines or on the radio or TV take on a whole new significance when they wind up right in the middle of it.

Every direct contact with the poorest of the poor brings us to focus deeply on our own life and vocation. I have already told you about Madonna House in Combermere, Ontario, Canada. It is some 300 kilometers (approx. 185 miles) north of Toronto. There a group of lay men and lay women, with a few priests as spiritual directors, live a community life of poverty, prayer and work. They have dedicated themselves to the Church by pronouncing the three evangelical vows. Every year, scores of young people go there in search of authenticity and the real significance of life. While less known than the French community of Taize, it provides a similar experience.

I have often asked myself how it is that so many young people consider it worthwhile to go to Madonna House to pray and work, or why they choose to remain there the rest of their lives. Every year, at least ten to twenty young men and women enter this form of committed lay apostolate. Certainly it is not a lifestyle for a person who cannot relinquish comfort and riches, or pride and self will. The food there is very plain though nourishing; the sleeping arrangements are separate, communal dorms for men and women; and a monastic program of prayer and work is strictly observed. It is a community life of one big Christian family. The respect and affection each staff member at Madonna House has for the others — as well as for every guest who knocks at their door — is both visible and palpable. A remarkable joy pervades everything. All of this can only be explained as a faithful expression of their unique calling.

About this special vocation, Catherine Doherty, Foundress of Madonna House, has said:

> The spirit of Madonna House is one of ardent zeal for the glory of God, the salvation of souls, and the restoration of all things in Christ through Mary. You have come here by the inspiration of the Holy Spirit to dedicate your life in this very humble apostolate, hidden like the Holy Family of Nazareth — unknown, unsung, utterly indistinguishable, outwardly, from the rank and file of everyday humanity — except for a cross.
>
> The second aim of this Apostolate is to restore man and his institutions to Jesus Christ through Mary in the lay apostolate by means of work in any phase of Christian reconstruction.
>
> This is the work that you do. But the way that you are going to do it depends on who you are. What you do matters — but not much! Who you are matters tremendously! (Originally this was a talk given at Madonna House on March 22, 1956. It is now a part of the Madonna House Constitutions.)

Miriam, one of the staff members, told me that she had come to this community after having found her true vocation in Calcutta. Searching aimlessly for meaning in her life, she had gone to Calcutta and worked for several months there in Mother Teresa's houses. How many of these "Meaning-of-Life" pilgrim stories I have heard from staff members and guests at Madonna House! Before finally winding up in this rather unique center for the lay apostolate, tucked away in a little village in the Madawaska Valley, many of these people followed labyrinthine paths in what we call "the world" — the world of money, desire for power, pleasure, selfishness and indifference to what goes on in the hearts of others.

These young people had grown disgusted with all the fine talk about justice and peace, love and God. Upset about their own inner poverty and lack of peace, they came to Combermere because they heard of a rather exceptional woman by the name of Catherine Doherty who had gone to work in the slums of Toronto in the '30s and who, afterwards, had gathered a group of people around her. This group called each of their houses, "Friendship House." Early in Catherine's work in Canada they began to be known as "Madonna House."

I spoke to you and your friends about them not long ago, Bren, when we were discussing your apparent dissatisfaction with the Church of your parents and grandparents where you no longer seemed to feel at home. I told you, "In order to understand God and the Church, you have to live and experience them. Go to live in the radical poverty of Madonna House for awhile and work on the farm there along with other young people from America, Asia, Europe and Africa. There you will experience God and the Church. Or save your money and spend your vacation in Calcutta with the Missionaries of Charity."

Now I have actually let myself ramble on about Madonna House, haven't I? But I actually did it on purpose, Brenda, because I can't help but compare the life commitments of Catherine Doherty's followers with those of Mother Teresa and marveling at their similarity! There are two formidable women who could show you what to do with your life in a head on confrontation with poverty — both your own and that of others! For some years now, young people set out regularly from Belgium and Holland for Calcutta. Most of them return radically changed. They have deeper insights into life, mankind and the Church. "In order to understand what love for one's neighbor is, you must see it lived. Every loving act brings you into contact with God," Mother Teresa says.

That means that charitable works are actually God's works. Not only because they are accomplished by His instruments, but also because they are marked by His presence, for God is Love. Let yourself be taken in by others in love, dear Bren. People who truly love their neighbor are witnesses of God. I don't have to convince you of this. For five years now you have worked in the intensive care unit of a large hospital. The manner in which you dispense medical care is of the utmost importance to your patients. They can feel and know when you treat them, not simply as "cases," but as people with a heart and the desire to be loved, people in whom God has His dwelling. Your nursing commitment in such a place as an intensive care unit forces you to contemplate the existence of God and the meaning of life.

In Calcutta, you can find this in a very exceptional context: the actuality of an unimaginable poverty and the purely evangelical character of the services that so many young people — lay volunteers and hundreds of young religious, Brothers and Sisters of Mother Teresa — render in the heart of this poverty. In their interpretation lies the answer to the fundamental questions nagging your generation. Mother Teresa says that our vocation consists in revealing God Who is Life and Love; in reflecting Him in words and deeds of love for others. However small these words and deeds may be, they reflect the beauty of the Triune God. We all thirst for this beauty. Do you believe that our present day Christianity is the answer to the hunger and thirst of mankind, or do we have to expect something else? In this Christianity, we may not, we must not be merely onlookers. We are co-responsible for the evangelization of the world.

That's why, dear Bren, we must be able — I as a priest, you as a lay person — to share Jesus' life in and through ourselves. How is it written in St. Luke's Gospel? "Go back and tell John what you have seen and heard" (7:22).

The many young people who come to work in Calcutta will return to their countries and tell what they have experienced here. But they must do it honestly and not be ashamed to mention Jesus. As Mother Teresa said to me after one of our conferences, "Father, our life is really very simple. You can formulate it like this: 'All that we do is for Jesus through Mary. Period.' "

"What does *period* mean?" I asked.

"That your heart must be simple and pure in order to live in the unconditional service of the poor for Jesus through Mary," she answered. Then she went on, "Without this simplicity and purity you will reason the reality of Jesus and His Mother into a dead thing. Your self-sufficiency, your selfishness and your intellectual pride will inhibit His coming to live in your heart, because *God cannot fill what is already full.* It's as simple as that."

I believe that she has hit the nail on the head. If you want to understand faith, you have to love Jesus. Once you know that He loves you, you will be willing to open your heart in order to let the Jesus living in you flow out to others too. Whoever experiences and lives this love will understand it. That's why the engagement of these young volunteers here is so very important. The more intensely they experience Jesus in their selfless service of the sick and those who are less fortunate, in their acceptance of a simple lifestyle and the practice of a deep prayer life, the more they will astound the world.

More than ever before, the world needs young witnesses to Jesus. Try to be one now in your nursing. Then your coming here next year, as I hope you will, to spend some time in volunteer work will only be an extension of this. Besides the volunteers that we've been talking about you see hundreds of religious here. Right now there are some 300 vivacious young women who are preparing themselves to live this kind of total self-renunciation with the poorest of the poor for Jesus' sake.

Not a day goes by that I don't find myself asking, "What can so inspire them to choose a life of prayer, poverty, and such a radical gift of themselves?" It is simply not true that these girls, who come from various parts of India and its neighboring lands, want to become religious in order to improve their social status, or that they are simply too naive to undertake something else. There are many highly qualified and educated young women among them. I asked several of them just why they chose this life. The answer rang out loud and clear: "Out of love for Jesus!"

It has to do with Him! One of the most noticeable and hopeful signs in our present day Church is the vocation boom in the many young Churches in the Southern Hemisphere. Mother Teresa mentioned this more than once during her most recent visit to Flanders. She told the group of young people, to whom she spoke quite frankly, that many of them should become priests and religious. She said:

I have received requests to send Sisters from 140 bishops around the world. That means that I must have 560 new vocations. Isn't it remarkable that the Missionaries of Charity already have six novitiates in the world? They are in Manila, Calcutta, Tabora (Tanzania), San Francisco, Warsaw and Rome.

There are two active groups, Sisters and Brothers, the arms and hands of Jesus. They prepare the way for the Lord. Finally, during the last few years, Priest-Missionaries of Charity, a small group of priests and seminarians have been formed. They are the heart pumping energy and inspiration to us because they bring the Eucharist to our communities and to the poor.

There are more than 2400 professed Sisters, approximately 600 in formation, plus 500 Brothers and 15 Priest-Missionaries of Charity. The Congregation has 284 houses in 75 countries. What all of these young people are looking for is the God Who is Love with Whom they want to love all people. That is why they are willing to sacrifice their lives. "Whenever they come," Mother Teresa said, "they tell me point-blank that they desire to leave everything in order to become everything for Jesus."

I can't possibly imagine, dear Bren, that there couldn't be more western youth who want to lead such a life.

After having spent so many years among the Cree Indians in the Far North of Canada, Fr. Roger Vandersteene, the Oblate Missionary from our own Flemish region, wrote:

A total surrender to God is something tremendous, something with incalculable possibilities which will ultimately blossom forth into the one joy — God! It is even more beautiful and more difficult than you can imagine. Remain open to Him. It won't always be easy, but it will always be worth it in a way that surpasses all I can say.

Because this is also my own personal conviction, Bren, I wanted to write to you openly and honestly. You stand on the threshold of a full, vibrant life. There are, already, so many people who wander aimlessly, unable to make fundamental decisions. Sadly, it is all too real a danger that they will simply wither away in meaningless existences. Whatever you finally do decide, do it for Jesus through Mary, so that the people entrusted to you may be happy.

I can't end this letter without mentioning that other great lady, Catherine Doherty, and the many questions young people asked her about the meaning of existence, questions which she answered with the witness of her life. She often said that our faith is a love story between God and man. We must, for our part, love Him passionately by loving other people. But she always said, too, that, in order to love with God's heart, we have to first empty our own.

As I meditated on George Suffert's book and the article in *Le Monde*, I have thought a lot about all of these things during my stay here in Calcutta. I thought of you, dear Bren, and your friends in Flanders, and of the volunteers and religious whom I meet daily in Mother Teresa's houses. Along with Suffert, I wanted to honestly and openly tell you in this letter what makes my heart so brimful of joy.

Read this letter in a free moment during one of your long night shifts in intensive care. I am actually "dying" to hear your reactions to it, as well as those of your friends. Give them my regards. Also don't forget to pass them on to your parents and brothers.

Lovingly,

Omer

WE DO IT FOR JESUS

To Eric, Arctic Missionary

Calcutta, December 22, 1987

Dear Eric,

I am sending you my New Year's wishes from Calcutta. By now, in Baker Lake in the Canadian Arctic, you will already be experiencing the dead cold of winter — temperatures of 35 to 40 degrees below (Celsius), 30 to 40 below (Fahrenheit), with the dusky moonlight of the long Polar nights. It is winter here, too, but the daytime temperatures are still 25 degrees (77° F.).

I was talking about you today, Eric, and that prompted me to write this letter. You will certainly recall that old missionary who sat next to you at the farewell party a year and a half ago. Together with 180 other missionaries from our diocese, our bishop presented each one of you with a missionary cross. One man remained seated, looking extremely exhausted. He could hardly move. He was Celest Van Exem from Elveringe, a village close to Ypres. He has been active in India for 50 years, most of which have been spent in Calcutta.

In the early afternoon, I went to visit him in St. Xavier's College infirmary where he is recuperating from a foot ailment. We have known each other since the early '70s when I first began accompanying groups of mission friends to India. We usually spent ten days or so in Calcutta. During Celest's last vacation in Flanders, we were together a lot. Often we talked about missions and missionaries. It was really he who insisted that I accept Mother Teresa's and Archbishop Henry's invitation to come to Calcutta to speak about the spirituality of Madonna House to the Missionaries of Charity, as well as to other groups of priests and seminarians.

Celest has been the spiritual director of many Sisters since the very beginning of Mother Teresa's foundation in 1950. It was he who helped her to discover and follow her true vocation back in 1944 when he became acquainted with her in the community of Loretto Sisters on Convent Road here in Calcutta. He used to say Mass there and give spiritual direction. This dynamic and intellectual Van Exem who, in the minds of his superiors, was destined to teach exegesis and set up an Islamic study center, actually became the great animator of one of the most important missionary institutes of our present day. He is one of the very few who, since the beginning of her apostolate, knew Mother Teresa so intimately and helped her so profoundly. Despite this, he has always managed to keep a low profile — simple and unobtrusive. During the years of his active work in one of Calcutta's most difficult parishes, Howrah, he lived among the poor and gave great help to the many Sisters who, in the meantime, had joined Mother Teresa. He inspired them with his wise counsel, his psychological insight, and the example of his detached and holy priestly life.

When I went to visit him today, I saw, on his table, the mission cross that he had received that night from our bishop. He seemed so happy and indicated what a pleasure that departure ceremony had been for him. He told me:

> The infection in my foot is the result of rat bites that I received during my time in Howrah. The doctor has now ordered me to stay in bed for several weeks. This gives me lots of time to pray, to read, to write and to receive people. The longer I am here the more I come to realize that we, as missionaries, are sent by the local Church in our native lands. It is thanks to the faith and devotion of my parents and family that I have my vocation. The dedication and generosity of so many priests in Flanders has helped me a great deal to become a Jesuit missionary. I can't say how grateful I am to them for that.

With Celest I prepared the meditation I will give to a second group of novices tomorrow. It is on the first line from Catherine Doherty's Little Mandate. Together we reflected on our missionary vocation and again recalled the send-off which the missionaries had received from West Flanders. It was in Poperinge on August 10, 1985. We also spoke about the young missionaries who were present, and that's how your name came up.

Celest is a missionary who knows how to apply theory to practice. He has remained a thinker, able to follow the changes in the Church and world affairs while never losing sight of the essential values. The first Constitution of the Missionaries of Charity was written by him. He mentioned this Constitution during our chat. Chapter II, Article 13 reads:

> We are called the "Missionaries of Charity." A Missionary is one sent with a mission — a message to deliver. Just as Jesus was sent by His Father, we too are sent by Him filled

with His Spirit to be witnesses of His Gospel of Love and Compassion in our Communities first, and then in our apostolate among the poorest of the poor all over the world.

As Missionaries we must be
— Carriers of God's love, ready to go in haste, like Mary, in search of souls,
— burning lights that give light to all men,
— the salt of the earth,
— souls consumed with one desire: Jesus, keeping His interests continually in our places where He has not walked before,
— fearless in doing the things He did and courageous in going through danger and death with Him, and for Him,
— ready to accept joyously to die daily if we want to bring souls to God, to pay the price He paid for souls,
— ever ready to go to any part of the world at any time,
— always ready to respect and appreciate unfamiliar customs of other peoples, their living conditions and language, willing to adapt ourselves if and when necessary,
— happy to undertake any labor and toil and glad to make any sacrifice involved in our missionary life.

When I first met Catherine Doherty, in Haifa, at the house of Archbishop Raya where she was visiting in 1972, we had a discussion about the concept of mission. Like a dove pulled out of a magician's hat, I conjured up a few missiological definitions, and Catherine laconically replied that she left all theological speculation about the different approaches to missiology and how mission should be carried out to the academicians. She made it clear that she felt that, first of all, her staff members must realize that being a missionary is unthinkable without realizing that love identifies itself with those whom it serves.

She writes, in a Staff Letter dated October 8, 1962:

> Nor are the mission teams of Madonna House to be concerned with what is known as the intellectual aspects of mission work, though we prepare our staff workers, and we hope to prepare them even better, with academic knowledge of many things. . . . Nevertheless, their weapons must always be: PAX and CARITAS.

> Also, by now all of us have realized that love identifies itself with those it serves. Therefore, no one must come to a mission as "Lady Bountiful," or "Lord Bountiful," but all must walk in grave humility with a heart filled with gratitude that one has been permitted to come and serve one's brothers and sisters in another part of the world.

Catherine Doherty sees this missionary life as a going to Bethlehem — a living in Nazareth by identifying ourselves with those we have come to serve. In explaining her Little Mandate — the first part of which is "Arise! Go!" — she explains:

> I understand that by going to my Bethlehem, my Nazareth, by identifying myself with the poor, by living their life, by living the Gospel without compromise, by loving always, by remaining little, I would be hidden as Christ was hidden in Nazareth. And I consider Nazareth, at the same time, as the be-all and the center of my vocation. (From an unpublished talk entitled *How the Little Mandate Came to Be*, given in 1968 at Madonna House)

It is striking that these words are exactly the same words that I read on your ordination card almost ten years ago, Eric. It was June 4, 1978, wasn't it? Your bishop at that time was Right Reverend Omer Robidoux, OMI, who came to your town, Roeselare, for the occasion. In the service of the mission for which he gave everything and suffered much by loving and identifying with those he served, this same bishop died along with three other missionaries in a plane crash in Rankin Inlet (so close to your own mission), on November 12, 1986.

"Go! I send you. You have a task to accomplish for the people. . . ." With these words of farewell you were commissioned to go forth as a priest to your Eskimos in the Arctic. Never, in your life as a young boy, could you have imagined that one day you would be going to the ice and snowfields of the North Pole, to be there a "bearer of God's Love." You now have quite a special challenge there, receiving your Inuits, counseling and guiding those who have problems with alcohol and drugs and suicidal depression.

Fr. Celest arrived in Calcutta with the conviction that his was to be a life of study and contact with the Islamic world. Instead he became Mother Teresa's counselor and the animator of her missionary congregation. You will already have discovered in your life as a missionary, Eric, that God never quite explains the vocation that He calls one to. He doesn't fill in the details. You never know just where He will send you or what it will demand in effort and sacrifice. But He stays at your side, all the same, helping and guiding you. It is only when we have answered His call and begun our pilgrimage, as Catherine Doherty expressed it, that we can begin to understand things better.

Mother Teresa could never have imagined that one day she would become world famous, and that so many important people would look up to her and listen to her every word. Eric, did you ever read the address she gave in Oslo, on December 10, 1979 when she was presented the Nobel Peace Prize? She spoke about God who is Life and Love, and about the Good News that we must bring to the poor. For all those present she read the Prayer of St. Francis: "Lord, make me an instrument of Your peace. . . ." It was this same prayer that she distributed to the more than a thousand people gathered for the General Assembly of the United Nations in New York. She did so that they might pray it along with her.

"This is the sort of wonder that Jesus can perform with His missionaries," she said to me. But these wonders that God performs through us are generally unexpected. Our Blessed Mother Mary, as a young girl, surely never dreamed that she was destined to become the Mother of God. She accepted God's call and became our mother as well as His. Being a missionary means undertaking a journey to experience the wonder of God's Love and to share it with others. It is a life full of adventure; a life that does not let itself be determined by exterior circumstances such as climate or milieu.

I have seen how you yourself feel utterly at ease when you go hunting with the Eskimos there in the Arctic, or when you bravely confront the harsh, polar weather. Celest, too, is so acclimatized to the humid, tropical life in this impoverished and utterly depressing milieu, that he would find it extremely difficult to re-adapt to our way of life in Flanders. But life in the missions must also be seen as an adventure into one's most intimate self.

Catherine Doherty wrote:

Our journey of life . . . should be a journey inward to meet the God Who dwells within us. It is a long journey, not in time, perhaps, but in effort. It is a journey of death, yet of life . . . a journey of strife that leads to peace, of pain that leads to healing, of sorrow that turns to joy. (*Journey Inward*, Alba House, NY, 1984)

In one of the most important letters that she ever wrote to her staff members, she said:

Each person who comes to Madonna House is, in a manner of speaking — or should be — "pregnant with God." Those who are not do not have a vocation to Madonna House. This "pregnancy" is a grace from God Himself. He gives them a desire for Himself. This becomes a "seed" within them, leading them to Mary and Joseph's Nazareth — Madonna House — there to dwell in hiddenness, humility, and hard work at little, daily tasks which, if performed with great love, would truly preach the Gospel loudly!

There are many places He could have led them: the vast deserts of the contemplative Orders, the rocky but beautiful, steep road of married life, the heights of priestly life, or that of the active religious Orders. And maybe each one called to these various vocations would also have to go to Nazareth — but not in the way of the Madonna House Mandate. For our Apostolate, Nazareth seems to be a very permanent place, spiritually speaking. Even Eddie and I have been led very mysteriously to live there like Mary and Joseph.

So, pregnant with Christ, chosen by Him, led by Him, people are brought to the Nazareth of Madonna House to give birth to Him and to allow Him to grow to His full stature. They live with the Holy Family, as Jesus lived with Mary and Joseph for many years.

For you, Eric, this world is Rankin Inlet in the Inuit settlement of Baffin Island. For Celest it is the poor who live in the parish of St. Francis Xavier on Bipin Behari Ganguli Street as well as the hundreds of Missionaries of Christ with whom he has daily contact here in Calcutta.

During his last visit home, where he had come to re-cuperate, Celest and I went to Ghent to visit Mother Teresa's Sisters. On the front of their house hangs a placard with the name of the congregation. In Flemish *charity* is translated literally as *neighborly love*. When Celest saw this, he promptly remarked: "That's not a good translation. Mission is more than love of one's neighbor or social work. Mission takes its origin from God's Love." This is how Celest regards the missionary congregation he helped to found, as well as his own missionary life. And so we were back again to the heart of our discussion about mission and missionaries.

"Our vocation consists in making God known, showing Him to all people. That means that we, in our words and administration of the sacraments, in prayer and concrete service of the poor, radiate the beauty of the Triune God in and through the community of the Church," he said.

Mother Teresa and Catherine Doherty both speak about mission as the adventure of God's Life and Love that, in and through us missionaries, will reach all mankind. Missionaries are called to carry out and radiate the sending that has its origins in the bosom of the Triune God Itself. Mother Teresa loves the prayer of Cardinal Newman: "Dear Jesus, help me to radiate Your splendor wherever I go. Flood my soul with Your Spirit and Life. . . ." All of this takes place in the emptying of self for service. Our life of service isn't carried on just to be of help to our neighbor, but rather all is done to serve the Jesus Who lives in him. Our vocation is to minister to Christ in others. With this vision, human successes and failures lose their importance. Mother Teresa says:

God doesn't ask that we succeed in everything, but that we are faithful. However beautiful our work may be, let us not become attached to it. Always remain prepared to give it up, without losing your peace. The work doesn't belong to you but to Jesus.

In Catherine Doherty's Little Mandate there are the words:

Love — love — love, never counting the cost.

Missionary work is a matter of love — love of God Who, in Jesus, with and through us, goes out to all people ("to the marketplace," as Catherine put it; "to Calcutta," in the words of Mother Teresa) no matter what it costs. What both really mean is that to be a missionary is to go to the hearts of the people, which is also the heart of one's own existence. Mission must also be understood in this sense. The mission is actually realized in the small, unimportant things of everyday life. It goes without saying that we do need thinkers and experts in the various areas of Church and pastoral life. The largest group of missionaries, however, is to be found in the rank and file of ordinary people caring for souls, and the love and service of neighbor that flows from this.

In past years I often accompanied Celest on house calls in Howrah. I would just go along with him to visit and listen to his poor people in their little homes. Once I also accompanied a group of Sisters who were going into the slums. As we walked along, they prayed their rosary in silence.

In the Congregation's Constitutions, which I have already mentioned, I noticed the following:

From the contemplation of Jesus in the Eucharist we go to a contemplation of Him in the distressing disguise of the poorest of the poor and so proclaim the word of God to them in the streets and in the houses of the poor. Therefore, a deep spirit of prayer and recollection of the divine Presence should pervade even our hours of direct personal presence among the poor. We shall go two by two praying the rosary and contemplating the word of God in the streets.

I remember Catherine Doherty once told me that on one occasion, while she was living in the slums of Toronto, she received the visit of a priest who was told by his doctor to take daily walks for his health. Catherine told him that, since he had to walk three miles a day, why didn't he walk through the slums where the people lived. She said that it would be a sign of hope to them.

At first he couldn't see this at all. He preferred to walk through a nice park. But he took her advice and, in his clerical garb, he walked daily through the slums amidst areas filled with communists; with believers and unbelievers. In the beginning, he drew some taunts and unkind remarks, but gradually the people came to welcome him and asked for his prayers for the ill. They also gladly accepted medals which he always carried on his person. He became known as a caring presence in their midst and accomplished a lot of good by being just that, a sign of hope.

Yesterday Mother Teresa again showed me her hand. "Look," she said, laughing. "Five fingers! Jesus said that what we do for our neighbor with our own hands we do for him." This, Eric, is our life as missionaries.

A few days ago, I participated in a departure ceremony in the Motherhouse on Lower Circular Road. It was extremely simple, but also extremely impressive. Young

Sisters were preparing to leave for their respective missions in India and other continents. The departing Sisters stood in the little courtyard together with the novices and other professed Sisters. Mother Teresa was in their midst. Before the grotto of Our Lady they sang the following beautiful hymn:

> O most pure and loving heart
> Of my Mother and my Queen
> Grant that I may love Thee
> Love Thee daily more and more,
> Love Thee daily more and more.
>
> God will take care of you, be not afraid,
> He is your safeguard, through sunshine and shade.
> Tenderly walking, wherever you go,
> He will not leave you to wander alone.
>
> God will take care of you, still to the end,
> O what a Father, Redeemer and Friend!
> Jesus will answer, whenever you call.
> He will not leave you, so trust Him for all.

Mother Teresa then laid her hands on each of the departing Sisters and sent them forth. As it happened, I accompanied some of them in the mini-bus that brought them to the station or the airport. They all had happy smiles on their beautiful, radiant faces. They were all joyful and in high spirits. And do you know what I thought of? A few years ago, Eric, we were sitting one evening in an igloo, outside the mission in Hall Beach. It was bitterly cold and you said: "I'll light a candle. It will give light and warmth. Go and sit next to the candle." Together we prayed Compline. You, too, looked radiant, joyful and at peace. Ever since then, this igloo-experience has remained symbolic for me.

Missionaries are like that little candle in the igloo. They give their lives to Jesus that His Light and Love will warm men's hearts.

On taking leave of Celest, I asked him to bless me. He signed my forehead with the cross. I want to be very open with you, Eric. It is out of pure joy that I write all this to you in the twilight of this year. The joy that I can read in the eyes and on the faces of Mother Teresa and her Sisters, of Father Celest and of all the missionaries that I have had the privilege of meeting here in Calcutta is the joy of Jesus Who so visibly lives in them all. It is this very same joy in your own missionary life that I wish for you in the coming New Year.

Pray for me and for all our missionaries that we "will do everything for Jesus." Pass on my greetings to your confreres: Mike in Igloolik, Robert in Hall Beach, and the catechists, Bartolemy and Sidonie in Pelly Bay.

Warmly yours,

Omer

LETTER X:
GIVE ME YOUR HEART

To Miriam, Madonna House Staffworker, Paris

Calcutta, December 25, 1987

Dear Miriam,

I wish you a Joyous Feast of Christmas! Even though this letter will reach you only after New Year's Day, I know our wishes for one another, today, are mutual.

Mother Teresa's Sisters in Ghent have been praying that my stay here in Calcutta will be fruitful. You have also been doing that, along with your sisters, Rejeanne and Mary Kay. I am sure that you are asking the Triune God, the Theotokos (the Mother of God), and Catherine Doherty, foundress of Madonna House, that we might be ever more deeply and intensely united to one another in God's life. In this prayer you have had a special thought for these two communities: the Missionaries of Charity who, in the spirituality of Mother Teresa, want to witness to the poor the mystery of Jesus' thirst for mankind, and the group of priests and lay people who belong to the spiritual family of Catherine Doherty who try to live the Little Mandate in the marketplaces of this world. During my stay here in Calcutta, I have tried to explain the Little Mandate to seminarians, priests and more than 400 Sisters of Mother Teresa as our chosen way to the heart of happiness, God Himself.

I spent Christmas Eve with the archbishop in one of the city's parishes. A few hundred Bengalese Christians and a handful of Europeans attended the night Mass. The familiar, Christmas atmosphere of our cold, western countries was absent: the frost, the snow, city streets strung with lights and decorated trees. And yet I could join in heart and spirit with the Christian community here in its faith-filled celebration of the Feast of Peace and Love. Peace and love are words that take on completely different significance in Calcutta than they have in Europe. But there are similarities, too.

I suspect that you attended the vigil in the Church of St. Leo - St. Giles. It is there that Catherine Doherty, at the age of 85, gave her last European lecture. It was on March 22, 1981. As you would guess, it was about her love affair with God.

She stayed in the parish of Notre Dame des Blancs Manteaux, in a rather dilapidated old house built against one side of the church. It is there that you live in a few simple rooms on the second and third floors. It is there that you pray and welcome those who come to you with their spiritual hunger. There also you direct people who want to spend some time in one or other of the *poustinia* rooms, fasting, praying and reflecting. Not long ago, a Parisian magazine described your Madonna House in the Rue l'Abbe Migne, 1, as "an oasis in the desert of a very large city."

You probably attended Midnight Mass in the parish church which is situated in the Jewish quarter, bordered on one side by several well-known shopping streets, and on the other by the porno district.

Here in Calcutta it can be chilly at night, but there in Paris it will be quite cold now. There won't have been many people present at the service in your church. But whoever lives a life of faith in Jesus there in your metropolis does it with the same fervor that I have observed here. The many destitute in Paris have certainly headed for one or the other of the "*restaurants du coeur*," "restaurants of the heart," as the needy call the many charitable soup kitchens that try to reach out to serve them there.

In both these worlds, the goodness and love of God for humanity has become visible. This is Christmas. In little, down-to-earth ways, we try to show the poor how much God loves them. But we, Miriam, also belong to these poor because we are all sinners. We are all empty vessels who need redemption and the fullness of God's Life and Love. Nourished and strengthened by this Life, we will engage in the task of creating a more human world, one of justice and peace for all.

We were called to live for Jesus through Mary in the service of the poor. This is the ideal held up to us by Mother Teresa and Catherine Doherty. This calling brought us to Madonna House in Combermere, or to one of the field houses such as yours there in the parish of Notre Dame des Blancs Manteaux. It led me here to Mother Teresa in Calcutta.

During the Midnight Mass, I stood between Archbishop D'Souza and Bishop Leander Da Costa, chancellor of the diocese and pastor of St. Thomas Parish. Leander is a fine man who looks at everyone and everything with the eyes of the Gospel.

A few days ago, he took me to the auditorium of the "Buntain Education Centre" in Park Street to hear the "1987 Songs of the Season." It was a musical drama entitled "This Is Christmas!" There were 150 actors and singers.

The production was organized and sponsored by the Assembly of God Church. I could scarcely believe my eyes. The audience was packed with well dressed people, and they followed the three-hour-long program with rapt attention. The presentation was of extremely high quality down to the very last detail. The technical side of it, from lighting to management, was nothing short of perfection.

"This must have cost a fortune!" I whispered to Leander.

"The Assembly of God Church has a good mission here," he said. "They do a lot of educational and charitable work. Its head is a sympathetic Canadian who knows how to raise the necessary funds. But you mustn't lose sight of the fact that most of those outstanding performers, dressed in such gala costumes and uniforms, come from the slums. Otherwise, this perfection-plus performance would induce us to forget, for a few hours, the hard reality of Calcutta and the real meaning of Christmas."

The program, with all the usual Christmas and New Year's wishes, was presented in a dazzling, Hollywood style. "This belongs to it, too," Leander remarked. "As long as we don't forget the essentials."

In 1984, one of our Madonna House priests, Father Emile Briere, wrote about those essentials. He said that the formulation and development of these at Madonna House went back to 1962 when rebellious youth, clergy and nuns began to visit them. I quote him now, as I did in my book, *As I Have Loved You* (Veritas, Dublin, 1988):

> Faced with this onslaught, Catherine, Father Cal and myself asked, "What do we center our lives upon at this moment of real crisis in the Catholic Church?" And the answer was, "The Essentials." That is: God is Love; God loves you; God is Father, Son, and Holy Spirit; God

revealed Himself and became man in Jesus Christ. Each
one of us can live out the various phases of the life of Jesus
at one time or another, and perhaps often within the space
of a few hours, such as Bethlehem — its helplessness;
Nazareth — its wealthy, rich, productive hiddenness in
the doing of simple things. (You will never go wrong by
following Nazareth. It will leave a glow upon your face
that will preach to our visitors more strongly than anything else.) You live His public life when you teach, when
you listen; His passion, His death and resurrection when
you undergo in your own heart, soul and flesh the totally
frightening darkness, helplessness and torture of His passion and death, and the glory of His resurrection. All this
within the mantle of Our Lady of Combermere, trusting
in her no matter what.

We realized, twenty-two years ago, that the extremely
sophisticated opinions which were being expressed by
various theologians could lead only to the total confusion
of the people of God. And so we determined with all of our
hearts to stress the essentials of love, of the Trinity, the
Incarnation, the passion and the death and resurrection
of Jesus, the presence of the Holy Spirit and of Mary in all
our lives to such an extent that people could find direction
or redirection for their lives; could rediscover faith; could
again place their trust in God, in Jesus the Lord, in Our
Lady and escape the confusion.

We have often spoken about these essentials during our
meetings with the Madonna House community there in
Paris and with Mother Teresa's Sisters who live close by.
Mother Teresa has also spoken to me a great deal about the
essential things during these days here. Her thoughts,
words and deeds always have Jesus as their starting point —
Jesus, the Son of a loving God who expressed on the cross
His thirst for the love of all men, and her desire that her

Sisters truly love one another with the love with which they love the God Who became man in the womb of the Virgin Mary, who is also our Mother. This is the essential thing. From the heart of this reality we approach others. In Jesus and through Mary, we form a community with them.

"Because God lives in us and makes us godly, we are one another's brothers and sisters — one big family of God's children," Mother Teresa said once again to me during our last talks. I know all too well that people can judge her words rather critically as not being sufficiently grounded theologically, or as being too childishly emotional. However, criticism really falls flat when one sees how she and her Sisters live these essentials of our lives and our faith in such a concrete way. I have already told you, dear Miriam, how much she likes to use insignificant things to convey deeper realities.

Yesterday, for example, she showed me a holy card with Christ as a prisoner with His crown of thorns. Anyone would say that it was a tasteless, devotional image of Christ covered with rather garish black and red wounds. Under the drawing are the words: "I looked for someone to console Me, but found no one." With a roguish, irresistible smile in her eyes, she added the final words to the message: "See that you are the one who does so," and offered me the card. This incident moved me more deeply than you can imagine.

You are familiar with Catherine's *poustinia*, next to her log cabin on the banks of the Madawaska River in Combermere. It is in this *poustinia* that she spent many nights in prayer. For hours at a time, she would lie prostrate on the wooden floor, covered with her black Russian cloak. Next to the naked cross, adorning the wall of the hermitage hangs a large copy of that same black and red blotched Christ. Catherine also wanted to be the one to quench the thirst of her Beloved and bind up His wounds. Whether Christ is suffering in the poor or on the cross it is exactly the same, Miriam. This is clearly stated in Catherine's Little Mandate:

> Arise — go! Sell all you possess. Give it directly, personally to the poor. Take up My cross (their cross) and follow Me — going to the poor — being poor — being one with them — one with Me.

A few years ago, I preached a retreat for the Missionaries of Charity in Ghent. Mother Teresa was also present. Following the final talk she gave me a reflection based on a text from St. Matthew that she herself had written in a hospital room in Rome, on June 19, 1982. She entitled it "Who Do You Say That I Am?" I compared this text with a prayer found, not long ago, in one of Catherine's diaries. It was written during the first years of her apostolate among the poorest of the poor and is dated August 20, 1934. Again, there is a striking similarity between the two writings. Catherine wrote:

> O Jesus, I want to love Thee so that I can make others see Thy beauty, that I can have a share in bringing the world back to Thee for Thou alone art its salvation! O Jesus, prostrate before Thee, I beg only for one gift: a blinding love of Thee; an all-consuming love of Thee; an all-embracing love of Thee; a supernatural love of Thee; a gentle love of Thee; a passionate love of Thee; a childish love of Thee; a love unto death of Thee; a love unafraid of martyrdom for Thee; a love of all Thy poor in Thee; a love of all Thy sick in Thee; a love of all strayed ones in Thee; a love of all sorrowful ones in Thee; a love of all lonely ones in Thee; a love of all tired ones in Thee; a love of all little ones in Thee; a love of all scoffing ones in Thee; a love of all sinners in Thee.

Jesus, my prayer is "make me love Thee more and more and love all men in Thee!"

Mother Teresa, filled with the same burning love for Jesus, meditated in her hospital room:

Jesus is the Word made Flesh.
Jesus is the Bread of Life.
Jesus is the Victim offered for our sins on the Cross.
Jesus is the Sacrifice offered at the Holy Mass for the sins of the world and mine.
Jesus is the Word — to be spoken.
Jesus is the Truth — to be told.
Jesus is the Way — to be walked.
Jesus is the Light — to be lit.
Jesus is the Life — to be lived.
Jesus is the Love — to be loved.
Jesus is the Joy — to be shared.
Jesus is the Sacrifice — to be offered.
Jesus is the Peace — to be given.
Jesus is the Bread of Life — to be eaten.
Jesus is the Hungry — to be fed.
Jesus is the Thirsty — to be satiated.
Jesus is the Naked — to be clothed.
Jesus is the Homeless — to be taken in.
Jesus is the Sick — to be healed.
Jesus is the Lonely — to be loved.
Jesus is the Unwanted — to be wanted.
Jesus is the Leper — to be washed clean.
Jesus is the Beggar — to be given a smile.
Jesus is the Drunkard — to be listened to.
Jesus is the Mentally Ill — to be protected.
Jesus is the Little One — to be embraced.
Jesus is the Blind — to be led.
Jesus is the Dumb — to be spoken for.
Jesus is the Crippled — to be assisted in walking.

Jesus is the Drug Addict — to be befriended.
Jesus is the Prostitute — to be removed from danger.
Jesus is the Prisoner — to be visited.
Jesus is the Old Person — to be served.

To me —

Jesus is my God.
Jesus is my Spouse.
Jesus is my Life.
Jesus is my Only Love.
Jesus is my All in All.
Jesus is my Everything.

Jesus, I love with my whole heart, with my whole being.
I have given Him all, even my sins, and He has espoused
me to Himself in tenderness and love.
Now and for life I am the Spouse of my Crucified Spouse.

Amen.

I was able to witness what these essential things mean to
us in Mother Teresa's house. I did so, Miriam, in the name
of our Madonna House family in Combermere and in the 22
mission houses in Canada, the United States, the Caribbean,
Brazil, Liberia, England and France where we strive to live
Catherine Doherty's Little Mandate. With the staff members, the young people in training, the priest directors, the
associate priests, and the deacons, we form a very small
group of 250 people in the worldwide Church who want to
live out the essentials of our faith in a humble way by being
faithful to the little things in our everyday life.

I have with me the article you wrote after your first visit
to Israel, the land of your fathers, and I shared it with those
whom I call "the saints of Calcutta" — seminarians, priests,
lay men and women, missionaries, religious, and Mother
Teresa herself. Born in Detroit, Michigan, you, a Jew, were

baptized in the chapel of Madonna House on December 21, 1969 after 22 years of searching. You joined the community as a staff member and were sent to the House of Prayer in Paris. There, thanks to the kindness of friends, you were given the opportunity to visit your people and the land where your roots lie. About this experience you wrote:

> And yet I have never felt so secure in my identity as a Christian. To live there as a Jewish Christian might be another story, but at this point, that wasn't the issue. On the contrary, it was as if God didn't want me to get caught up in complexities. As if He were saying: "Don't even try to pull it all together. Just stand before Me and pray."

> Maybe it is because in MH we try so hard to live what is essential and not get distracted by anything else that this could happen. I was aware that my experience was the result of all that I have lived at MH, and all that we live together. It was an experience of standing close to the heart of things, the awesome mystery of *Emmanuel*, God in our midst. (*Restoration*, February 1988)

Calcutta, the city of joy and the city of saints, with the almost legendary presence of Mother Teresa and her Missionaries of Charity, has given me the same realization as you had during your stay in Israel. It is as if Jesus also had said to me: "You mustn't try to understand everything here and decipher it with your rational, western mentality. I am here. Live in Me and let Me go to the poor of the world through you, together with My Mother and yours."

Last December 8, the Feast of the Immaculate Conception, I was present at the ceremony in the Motherhouse, during which quite a few Sisters either renewed their vows or pronounced their perpetual ones. On the same day at Madonna House, in the chapel in the woods, 15 young people dedicated their lives to God in obedience, poverty and chastity and pledged themselves in a special way to the Church and to Our Lady, the real Mother of our family. They received a small metal cross with the words *Pax* and *Caritas* engraved upon it. The members of Madonna House are given this cross when they first make their temporary promises.

Do you know, dear Miriam, that this day was deeply meaningful to me. I thought to myself: "In the making of promises and in the receiving of new assignments at Madonna House today we are joined in a very profound way to one another. We — this small, little-known group of lay apostles along with this large and ever-growing group of approximately 3,000 Missionaries of Charity under the charismatic leadership of Mother Teresa — never cease to amaze the whole world. During the ceremony of the pronouncing of vows in the chapel of the Missionaries of Charity, I prayed that Catherine Doherty's holiness and the spirituality of her Little Mandate might mutually influence the prayers, sacrifices and works of the Sisters here and throughout the world."

In everything that I have heard and seen during my encounters with Mother Teresa and her congregation, I have become more and more convinced that we will never be able to experience the essential things if we do not give Mary room in our hearts. If we take her hand we will taste the harmony and inner peace that are necessary to carry out the little things in an exceptional way for love of God. As the Little Mandate enjoins us, we are to "Do little things exceedingly well for love of Me."

"As a priest you must always hold Mary's hand in yours," Mother Teresa told me. "With her, you will become a holy priest." How much she liked to point to Jesus Who, while dying on the cross, said to His Mother that she must take John as her son and, in him, all of us as her children. "John was a priest," she reminded me, "and you priests must also care for Mary, as this was Jesus' wish on the cross. . . ."

You know that she named the House of the Dying *Kalighat Nirmal Hriday* — The Place of the Pure Heart. It is the house where they who were otherwise destined "to live and die as animals on the street, alone and unloved, can die as angels, encircled with love, tender care and affection." Our Lady is, for Mother Teresa, God's Nirmal Hriday — God's own "Place of the Pure Heart." Because her heart was so very pure, God wanted to become a man in her. Mary embodies all that Nirmal Hriday means. She is the resting place for God's love for humanity and His compassion; the temple, arrayed in poverty, so that God can be her only beauty. She is covered with humility so as to be exalted only in and by Jesus. It is Mary who protects our poverty, keeps us safe from despair and consoles us at our death. She opens her heart for us as the doors of Nirmal Hriday. There we can experience the strength of Jesus. As Nirmal Hriday is, so is Mary, a sign of hope and peace in a tumultuous world. She is a consolation for those who suffer; a radiant beauty in the drab disguise of our inner poverty. In her we find the Promise of new life and, above all, the assurance that God never abandons us to our lot.

So we, too, are capable, not only of dying as angels but also of living for others. Nirmal Hriday is, indeed, the image of Mary's own heart, God's first Nirmal Hriday. This image, dear Miriam, is the one we must pass on to one another, to all our brothers and sisters in Madonna House. Because we belong to that House, it is laid upon us to set forth her own mystery by nestling close to her. In this way, we, too, will become "places of the pure heart" both for God and for those who come to us with their hunger and their thirst.

Every day here in the houses of Mother Teresa in Calcutta, as well as in all of her houses around the world, a truly beautiful prayer is addressed to the Mother of God, one composed by Mother Teresa herself. It made me think of the hymn we sing daily in the Madonna House chapel when we pray to Mary for all the staff members of the various mission houses:

> Rejoice, Virgin Mary, full of grace!
> O Theotokos, the Lord is with you.
> Blessed are you among women,
> And blessed is the Fruit of your womb.
> For you have given birth to the Savior of our souls.
>> (From an old hymn entitled: *Rejoice, Virgin Mary*
>> [*Bohorodice D'Ivo*])

Mother Teresa prays in the same way with her Sisters:

> Mary,
> Mother of Jesus,
> give me your heart,
> so beautiful, so pure,
> so immaculate,
> so full of love and humility,
>> that I may be able to receive Jesus in the Bread of Life,
>> love Him as you loved Him
>> and serve Him in the distressing disguise of the
> Poorest of the Poor.   Amen.

How happy I am that I could write this, my last letter in Mother Teresa's house, to you. This is also Our Lady's house. She will purify our hearts and prepare them to be the dwelling places of the Triune God. Share the message I send you, Miriam, with all at Madonna House in Combermere when you go there for the meeting of all the local directors.

I have only a few hours left before Bishop Leander comes to take me to the airport for my trip home. I will use this time to thank the archbishop for all he has done for me and to pop in quickly to see Father Celest Van Exem, S.J. They have both done so much to make my stay here such a pleasant one.

Yesterday I took leave of Mother Teresa. I gave her my priestly blessing and she gave me a card with a photo of her holding a starving child. On it she wrote: "Try to be everything for Jesus through Mary. Let us be as small and humble as Mary, in order to become as holy as Jesus. Let us pray for this. Mother Teresa."

This morning she phoned to wish me a safe trip and to invite me to return to preach several retreats for her Sisters. A few hours ago, around noon, two novices came with a note. It reads:

Dear Father O. Tanghe,

God love you for all the love you shared with us all during the three days. All our Sisters and myself thank you for what you gave us.

Pray that we live up to that and allow Jesus to love in us and, through us, all we come in contact with.

Keep praying for us that we give only Jesus to all with whom we come in contact.

Thank you — our gratitude to you is our prayer for you.

God bless you.

M. Teresa, MC

I know, dear Miriam, that she will also continue to pray for our Madonna House Family. Isn't this the most beautiful Christmas gift I can give you and your sisters in Paris, Rejeanne and Mary Kay? In a few days I will call you.

Merry Christmas and a Blessed New Year!

Father Omer

Madonna House Associate Priest